CW01021881

DON'T WASTE YOUR TEARS

Dedication
To all the friends in tears in the whole world,
with whom I make a toast with the cup of suffering.

Thank you
to Maria de Lourdes Delgado,
Denis and Marlene Barrett for their generous and
free work in translating the book;
to Isabel Hermes, my dear "English mouth" in Brazil
for all contact made with the translators and editors
of this book.

JORGE TADEU HERMES

Don't Waste Your Tears

Edited by
Denis & Marlene Barrett

ST PAULS

Original title: *Não jogue fora suas lágrimas*
Translated from Portuguese by M. de Lourdes Delgado and
Denis Barrett.

ST PAULS Publishing
187 Battersea Bridge Road, London SW11 3AS, UK
www.stpauls.ie

ISBN 978-0-85439-734-1

Set by TuKan DTP, Stubbington, Fareham, UK
Printed in Malta by Progress Press Company Limited

ST PAULS is an activity of the priests and brothers
of the Society of St Paul who proclaim the Gospel
through the media of social communication

CONTENTS

introduction

[epigraph line, illegible]

Weeping ... it is something with which we are all familiar. It is a common experience. "While of tears ..." these words from the prayer to Our Lady ... There is more weeping than laughter in this world. We cry because we are hungry, or because we lack necessities, or because we cannot find work. We cry because of wars and injustice, or because we are lonely. We cry because of sickness, or the death of a loved one. We cry because of a crisis in our marriage, because our family has broken up, or because someone is addicted to alcohol or drugs. We cry because of separation and abandonment; we cry because we have been betrayed by a friend or by someone we love. We cry when we are falsely accused or slandered; we cry when our good name is blotted. We cry because of our longings, our pain, or our love. In a word, in any and every way that we suffer, we cry because of the pain we feel.

What is the use of tears? Do we shed them in vain, onto the void, all for nothing? Are our tears ...

Introduction

To you do we send up our sighs, mourning and weeping in this vale of tears.

Weeping: this is something with which we are all familiar. It is a common experience. "Vale of tears": these words from the prayer to Our Lady say it all. There is more weeping than laughter in this world. We cry because we are hungry, or because we lack necessities, or because we cannot find work. We cry because of wars and injustice, or because we are losers. We cry because of sickness, or the death of a loved one. We cry because of a crisis in our marriage, because our family has broken up, or because someone is addicted to alcohol or drugs. We cry because of separation and abandonment; we cry because we have been betrayed by a friend or by someone we love. We cry when we are falsely accused or slandered; we cry when our good name is defiled. We cry because of our longings, our pain, or our loss. In a word, in any and every great loss that we suffer, we cry because of the pain we feel.

What is the use of tears? Do we shed them in vain, into the void, all for nothing? Are our tears merely a sign of weakness – men who are really men don't cry? No! A manly man does cry. He cries because he is a man. He cries because he is human. Those that do not know how to cry become cold and repressed. Tears are tremendously, immensely, important. How they heal! But if our tears are to be blessed, it is necessary to "learn" how to cry (Matthew 5:5; Psalm 126:5,6).

Praise God, I am a man who cries. Rather: I am a man, and I cry. I cry a great deal. Sometimes I ask myself if there isn't a flowing spring of tears within me, for otherwise I couldn't say where all those tears come from.

I was called upon once to preach a retreat to the Catholic community Boa Nova of Recife. A few days before the retreat, they asked me to preach about the suffering that heals. My immediate response was, "a very good theme!" – in fact the retreat was already prepared in my heart, harvested in the labour of my life during a time when I experienced great suffering, I lived through it then and it is still with me today. All I had to do was open my lips and speak. That was where the inspiration for this book was born.

Before I wrote in ink anything that I offer you in these pages, it had already been written in blood and made fruitful by many tears.

Ah! Jesus cried with me. The Blessed Virgin Mary, and many friends, cried with me as well.

I pray that God will teach you to cry, for there are many blessings in tears. But it is necessary to know how to cry, for otherwise your tears will be wasted.

Chapter 1

Blessed be suffering

Blessed be God, and blessed be all the ways that brought me to him. Blessed be suffering. Yes, blessed be suffering.

Maybe you'll think that I am exaggerating, but I am not. Blessed be suffering. Let us give glory to God for all the mystery of pain, all the failures and persecutions, all the cruel and dishonest things people say of us and all the nasty surprises that the world springs on us. Blessed be God.

We are all alike – but in what are we alike?

If there is anything in which all of us human beings are alike, it is what we call suffering.

Clearly we are alike not because we all enjoy a high standard of living, good health, many friends, or because we are famous or enjoy great prestige, but rather because in some way all of us are in need. It is that need, the lack of something necessary, that makes us all alike. Pain, tears and suffering are well known to every one of us.

"I have seen... I have heard..."

Everyone suffers. Does this mean that God is not concerned, has nothing to say about it – about the suffering we all experience? It is obvious that he does have something to say. It would take me a long, long time to remind you of all the passages in the Bible about suffering. For example, see what God says in Exodus 3:7-8: "I have seen the miserable state of my people in Egypt, and I have heard their appeal to be free of their slave-drivers. Yes, I am well aware of their sufferings, and I mean to deliver them..."

God knows how we suffer, and he doesn't fold his arms. By the incarnation of the Word, he literally came down to deliver us. Jesus truly suffered our pains with us: "His state was divine, yet he did not cling to his equality with God, but emptied himself to assume the condition of a slave and became as men are; and being as all men are, he was humbler yet, even to accepting death, death on the cross" (Philippians 2:6-8).

No one in the entire universe has suffered more than God himself. Jesus suffered all the torment of Calvary in order to redeem humanity; he suffered rejection, people told malicious lies about him, slandered him, tried to take away his good name; he suffered the traitor's kiss from one of his most intimate friends. He suffered the envy of the religious people of his time; he suffered attacks from the powers of darkness, and he suffers still for every one of us, interceding for us before the Father.

He cried over Jerusalem, and he goes on crying over our hard, closed hearts – our hearts that refuse to open up, let go and turn completely to God.

Is suffering good for anything?

Let's be honest – if suffering was good for nothing in our life, God would have done away with it long ago. And also, between ourselves, if the devil served no purpose at all in God's plan for our salvation, God would have done away with him long ago. You can be sure of this, because God does not love suffering, nor does he take pleasure in making people suffer. The devil doesn't know it, but he is in fact working for God. How many people hasn't he already driven to God? He torments a person beyond endurance, and that person runs straight into God's arms. It is obvious that the devil destroys a great deal. How many people have been left with their lives totally wrecked, a real hell. But among those, how many there are that this same devil has driven to God. It is very true. God has so many ways and uses so many means to win us over, to heal us, to draw us to him and to save us. And if we suffer in ways that he doesn't heal, it is because he is using them to bring about the healing of other sufferings in our lives.

Truly, the sufferings that God doesn't take from us are the very ones that he uses to deal with other ills we suffer. How many of us turn to God because of our suffering! If it were not for the suffering we have endured, where would we be today? Blessed be God for the mystery of suffering. Blessed be God for this truth.

In chains

Saint Paul calls himself a messenger-in-chains of the Good News. As he says in the letter to the Ephesians (6:20), he is an ambassador in chains. Paul, the greatest preacher in the history of the Church, a missionary who went 'to the ends of the earth', spoke about himself as an ambassador in chains for Christ. The ambassadors of Christ still carry out their mission in chains: under persecution, in spite of opposition, bearing the difficulties this world puts in their way.

Blessed be God for the chains that the world puts upon us. That is how we are given the credentials to preach the gospel. Blessed be suffering! Blessed be God for suffering!

I would like to share with you my thoughts on four Bible passages about suffering that have made a deep impression on me. Let us now look at each of them closely.

The need for tribulation

Having preached the Good News in that town and made a considerable number of disciples, they went back through Lystra and Iconium to Antioch. They put fresh heart into the disciples, encouraging them to persevere in the faith. 'We all have to experience many hardships', they said, 'before we enter the kingdom of God' (Acts 14:21-22).

Let me stress the words "have to": we have to experience many hardships before we enter the kingdom. This tells us that hardships are something necessary for our salvation.

What do we mean when we say something is necessary? We mean that we cannot do without it: to live, we must have it. Our life is made up of many things, some of them are important, and some are necessary. Is nourishment merely important? No, it is absolutely necessary. To drink water – is that important? Even more than nourishment, it is necessary. If there is no water for you to drink, you will die. Sleeping in a comfortable bed – is that necessary? No. It is important, and it is good, but it is not necessary, because you can sleep on the floor. You can indeed go to sleep on the bare floor if you have no bed. Do you understand the difference between something that is important and something that is necessary? Some things are important, and some are necessary. You cannot ever do without the ones that are necessary.

Jesus said to Martha that Mary wanted the one thing necessary: to be his disciple (Luke 10:38-42). We have many important things to do: some, we have to do right away, yet many we can leave for tomorrow. But to be a disciple of Jesus is something that must be for now, at this very moment.

Carrying the cross of Jesus – is that something important? No, it is necessary. You cannot follow Jesus without the cross. There is no other way to follow him. To enter into the kingdom of God we have to experience many hardships, and therefore hardships are necessary. We must be born again in a spiritual way: in that birth there is no anaesthetic, no caesarean: we cannot be born spiritually without labour pains.

The narrow door

Jesus said that the door that leads to the kingdom of God is narrow. The door that leads to the kingdom of God is like this: as you approach the doorway to go in, it is narrow, but as it opens out into the kingdom, it is wide. The door that leads to perdition is the opposite. As you go in it is wide, but as you pass through, it becomes crushingly narrow. At the bottom the crush turns everyone into mush, no 'livers', only 'pâté'! The doors of the world open wide, very wide, swallowing everyone that passes through them. Sin, permissiveness, vice, the customs of the age, the media – TV, cinema, papers, glossy magazines, and all the rest – help to widen these doors: "Come, come. Do whatever you want – enjoy life!" And many are lured by the invitation to go in, and eventually to be crushed and die. But the way into the kingdom of heaven is narrow at first; as you move in it becomes wider and wider, opening the way to eternal happiness. Cardinal Newman used to pray, "Lord, the door is too narrow and I am too big. But since the door cannot be made wider, help me to become smaller, so that I may pass through".

It is necessary to enter the kingdom of heaven

through many hardships. It is necessary to enter through the door of conversion, of a change in the way we live: it is necessary to choose a healthy diet, to shed our spiritual fat and so be able to enter the kingdom of God.

This is one way that suffering comes to help us: it gives us the chance to become spiritually fit and lean, so that we can pass through the narrow door. Sometimes, as we fight against it, we get hurt: our pride is broken, and we bash our nose against the wall. When you've bashed your nose, you can't be puffed up any longer, and you are able to go through the narrow door.

Butterflies

I always like to watch the ways of natural things. One thing especially I love to see is how a butterfly comes out of the cocoon. You know that the butterfly starts as a caterpillar; the caterpillar spins a cocoon around itself and then changes inside. The butterfly is delicate, the cocoon very hard. The butterfly has a difficult job to get out, because the fibre of the cocoon is very tough, compared with the fragility of the butterfly.

Inside, the butterfly turns and twists, twists and turns, turns and twists, until she breaks the cocoon and is able to fly away. While she is turning and twisting inside the cocoon, she is strengthening her muscles, and that is exactly why she is able to fly. If trying to give a little help to the butterfly you break the cocoon to let her go, she will never be able to fly, because her exertions in breaking out of it herself give her the strength she needs to come out flying. Nature is very beautiful, but she does not make it easy for the butterfly to get out of the cocoon. She has to get out by herself, because the very difficulty of her struggle and anxiousness to get out gives her strength and prepares her wings so she can come out flying.

What we learn from the butterfly, we can apply to our own lives. We go through certain problems and experience certain difficulties that we alone must solve. Nobody can solve them for us. If somebody else does take over and solves them for us, we will be left weak, handicapped, and we will never be able to "fly" in life. How much it is part of our life, and how important it is for us, that we learn what it is to twist and turn in our cocoon!

All of us have a cocoon: a difficulty, a problem, a crisis, a sin that we are struggling against. A cocoon is not a place where we get killed in a struggle; it is a place where we exercise our wings so that we can come out flying. If I go and break open your cocoon, I will spoil the chance you have and you will never be able to fly. And if you try to solve all my problems, you will be spoiling my chances. Do you know that? If you try to solve all my problems for me, you are spoiling me, not loving me, because I will become a cripple, too weak to take control of my own life.

The parable of the prodigal son (Luke 15:11-32), describes this situation very well: the father suffered tremendously while the son was living with the pigs. Yet he didn't go and fetch him. He left him there to come to his senses and become aware that he was living among pigs and like a pig. He left him to decide for himself to get up and go back to his father's home. When he did get up and go, the father ran to welcome him. Yet he waited for the son's initiative. It was the son who, inside the cocoon, came to his senses and recognised that it was no use remaining in that place of struggle. Suppose the father had gone to him in the midst of his trouble and got his son out of the pigsty before he had seen for himself that the pigs did him no good – the son would have brought all the "pigs" with him into his father's home. The father allowed the process to take place in the life of his son, and it was only then that the son could realise where he was and to decide to come back to his father's home. Only after that could he receive his father's embrace. He was on the way, still far away, when the father went to meet him. A sign of his willingness alone was sufficient – "I really want to get out of here" – for the father to go and meet him and help him.

Give thanks to God: "blessed be the suffering that makes me find strength to learn to fly. Blessed be the suffering that helps me to come to my senses and that gives me courage to get up."

False crosses

It is important for us to know that many of our sufferings don't give glory to God.

A habitual alcoholic carries a cross, yes – a tremendous cross. Is it Jesus' cross? No, that one comes from the devil. That cross should be thrown away, because it is destroying that person's life. If you have hatred in your heart you suffer, clearly – and how you suffer! Is it a cross? Yes, and a very heavy one. Is it Jesus' cross? No. That cross you should throw away, because it does not glorify God. On the contrary, it is a blasphemy against God.

Does a drug addict suffer? Very much! Is it a cross? It is, and a very heavy one. Does it glorify Jesus? No. You have to find a way to throw that cross away.

From some crosses we must free ourselves as quickly as possible. The cross of hatred, the cross of vice, the cross of sin, the cross of our self-loathing, and other crosses that don't give glory to God. These have to be thrown into the fire as quickly as possible.

A glorious grace

He has given you the privilege not only of believing in Christ, but of suffering for him as well (Philippians 1:29).

Here St Paul is saying that we receive two great graces from God. The first grace: to believe in Christ; a marvellous grace. Without faith, what would become of us? And the second grace: to suffer for Christ. It is a gift, it is a grace, it is a present from our Father.

Maybe what I am going to say now will come as

20

a shock to you, but it is pure truth. To suffer for Christ is not a punishment but a privilege: it is a gift, it is an honour. The greatest glory that anyone can receive on the face of the earth is to suffer for Christ, to be humiliated and persecuted for believing, to suffer failure, contradiction, opposition, to be laughed at and mocked by society for believing in Christ and for loving Christ. None of these things are reason for us to be ashamed, to go about with heads hanging low, to feel we are losers. These things are reason for us to give glory to God. To suffer for Christ is a gift. The greatest proof of love is to suffer for the one you love. Jesus himself said: "a man can have no greater love than to lay down his life for his friends" (John 15:13). To suffer for Christ is the greatest honour that anyone can have in this life.

When we begin to understand this, we will say with all sincerity in the depth of our heart before Jesus: "Lord, I am not worthy of this suffering, I am not worthy of this glory".

The apostles came away from the Great Council, the Sanhedrin, glad to have had the honour of suffering for the sake of the Name (see Acts 5:41). They were whipped and they came away with backs on fire because of the scourging, but with hearts exulting for joy. They went out happy for having been worthy to suffer torments for the name of Jesus. To suffer for Christ is an honour, the highest honour that anyone can have on the face of the earth.

Martyrdom

To suffer martyrdom… Maybe you think: "Martyrs are the giants of faith". Without a doubt, martyrs are champions of faith. Yet there are two types of martyrdom, and both are very beautiful in God's eyes. One of them is the martyrdom of being condemned unfairly: they take a Christian and crucify him, burn him, throw him in a cauldron of boiling oil, throw him to the wild beasts… That is one kind of martyrdom. But there is another, more common kind of martyrdom that day by day gives you a dose of suffering for following Christ. Are you not then giving your life for him? Yes, you are, it is obvious. It is a martyrdom of merit and of inestimable value.

There are some people who are worthy of dying for Christ. There are others who are worthy of not dying for Christ: their life is a living, daily martyrdom as they struggle against themselves, against their bad inclinations, against vice that is always knocking at the door of their heart, against sin that every day invades their life. Some struggle day by day to remain faithful to Jesus in the midst of a complicated family situation. Some remain always faithful to Christ though they have to live and survive on a small salary that is not enough for their basic needs. Or even worse, some can find no work and how difficult it is for them to survive. This is a martyrdom of inestimable value; embraced in that spirit, it glorifies God in a tremendous way.

Every one of us is called to martyrdom, to give our life to Christ. Some have the grace of being martyred right away – thrown into the lion's den and quickly devoured. Others are found worthy of not dying for Christ all at once like that, but instead little by little every day, witnessing, declaring by the life they live that their hearts are centred in God. Such a life "would be a sign from God that he has given you the privilege not only of believing in Christ, but of suffering for him as well" (Philippians 1:29) – now there is a reason to glory, a reason for honour, a reason to rejoice greatly in our heart.

Test your faith: does it make you uncomfortable?

"You are well aware, then, that anybody who tries to live in devotion to Christ is certain to be attacked" (2 Timothy 3:12).

Everyone who wants to live a life devoted to Christ will suffer persecution: every one, and not just a few. In other words, anyone who lives an authentic and devoted Christian life will suffer, will have to endure pain and persecution for the cause of Christ, because a faithful disciple of Jesus makes people uncomfortable!

For sure, a Christian will make people uncomfortable, because of the way he lives: he will be meek; his criteria, his values, and the principles that he lives by and defends are so different from theirs. Such a person is a distinct shock to the mentality and culture of his time. A youngster today who wants to live chastely makes many other youngsters uncomfortable, because they don't live chastely. He is a real shock to them. He is like a pebble in their shoe. He doesn't need to say anything: simply by not going to bed with a girlfriend, he is already talking very loudly, and those who have no scruples about doing that kind of thing hear him very clearly. He doesn't even need to speak about Jesus; he just needs to live his holiness. He makes them uncomfortable by his way of being. They say, "Everybody goes to bed with their girlfriend or their boyfriend". "Oh yes?" he answers. He doesn't need words: his behaviour says, "I am not going with mine. Why? Because my body is a temple of the Holy Spirit and I want to keep my life a place of holiness." As the great monk, St Anthony, (250–356) once said, "A time will come when men will lose their mind, and when they see someone who has not lost his mind they will say, 'You are crazy, you are not like us'."

Do you understand? Live cleanly and you'll be called mad!

Married people who live in fidelity don't need to open their mouths to speak about Christ to those who live in adultery: these will feel accused by their own conscience.

A faithful disciple of Christ will always provoke reaction in his surroundings. Everyone who loves to live in a way that is true to Christ will have to suffer persecution. A priest who wants to be faithful to his mission and to his Lord will make people very uncomfortable, and he will suffer very much. Suffering will come to faithful people from all sides, from inside the church and from outside. They will suffer calumny; people will attack their good name; they will suffer pressure…

To make olive oil, you have to press olives – and the harder you press the olives, the more the oil flows. To make wine, it is necessary to press the bunch of grapes. The harder you press, the more the wine flows out. A servant of God once said that pain is the winepress of the soul, causing the best wine to flow.

Jesus in Gethsemane sweated blood. Gethsemane was like an oil-press: Jesus suffered his agony there. He started feeling the pressure there in Gethsemane, pressed so that he would yield the best oil. It is the same with our life: the more profoundly the pressure is on us, the more the good wine will flow from our soul, the more we will yield the pure oil. If we want to live faithfully in Christ Jesus we are already in the soul-press, where our life will be yielding the best oil even while it is being purified of everything that is not good.

But doesn't Jesus heal our pains?

Maybe you will ask: "Fr Jorge, but doesn't Jesus heal our pains?" It's obvious that he does heal! And how he heals! How many graces he gives and how many miracles he performs! It is precisely in our pains and needs that he manifests his saving love.

Yet we must be honest: are there many who are healed by Jesus? Yes, there are. But are there many who are not healed by Jesus? Yes, there are many. Are there many who have cancer and ask Jesus to heal them and they are healed? Yes. And are there many who have cancer and ask to be healed but are not healed? Yes, there are, it is true. There are many who have family problems and ask Jesus, and are the problems all solved? Yes. And are there many who have family problems and ask Jesus, and it seems that nothing is resolved? Yes, they are also many!

Those "who are not heard" – are they less loved by Jesus, or excluded by him? Definitely not! Don't be upset when you feel angry with God when it seems that your prayers are not heard, because when Jesus doesn't heal a problem it is because that very problem is resolving other problems. It is bringing healing, giving the solution to other problems.

Let me repeat what I just said: I am convinced that when Jesus doesn't provide the solution to a problem, it is because that problem is providing the solution to other problems!

I see servants of God who have a tremendous healing ministry. God uses them to heal the blind, help paralytics get up, raise the dead. But even so they have their own problems and they die of things like cancer.

Fr Tardif, for example, died while preaching a retreat. Who didn't know Fr Tardif's ministry, his preaching, and his gift of healing? What a tremendous person, used by the power of God to heal many people all around the world!? He died of a heart condition, while preaching a retreat to priests.

God has his purpose; God has his ways; God has his means of sanctification. Therefore, don't be angry and bitter when it seems that your prayer is not being answered. Jesus is listening. He is working in a marvellous way that will surprise and move you greatly when you come to see it. The ways of God are perfect, they are straight, just, and their outcome proves them right!

Should we ask for healing? Always, always – Jesus always heals – always, but always in his way. He always resolves problems in his way, for our greater benefit and for the greater glory, honour and praise of his wisdom.

Do the friends of Jesus also suffer?

"There was a man named Lazarus who lived in Bethany … and he was ill" (John 11:1).

Do you know who Lazarus was? He was the brother of Martha and Mary, and one of the best friends of Jesus.

Wait a minute – do the friends of Jesus also get sick? Do they also die? Yes. Jesus' friends also get sick. They also face problems. Jesus' friends also become bankrupt in their business. Friends of Jesus also face family problems. Friends of Jesus also die!

Nowadays we hear a false theology of prosperity proclaimed, different from the true theology of prosperity. The false one says that the friends of Jesus enjoy the best life, plenty of comfort, up-market homes, good health, lots of money in the bank, plenty of friends, marvellous children, a husband that is the envy of other women, a wife who is the best that nature could provide…

Friends of Jesus, says the false theology of prosperity, don't suffer because Jesus has suffered for us on Calvary. Is it true that he has already died for us on Calvary? It is true. Has he already dealt with pain once and for all on Calvary? Yes, he has. Did he take on himself all suffering on Calvary? Yes, he did. Did he defeat the devil? Yes, he did that too. But the friends of Jesus share in his own life, and he says that to follow him it is necessary for us to take up the cross. If someone wants to follow Jesus without carrying the cross, that person is not worthy of him.

"Lazarus who lived in Bethany… was ill." Lazarus is one of the people of the Bible who would seem less likely to become ill, because he was a friend of Jesus. He received Jesus in his own home; he used to have conversations with Jesus, exchanging ideas with Jesus. He is surely one of those less likely to become sick, and yet he did.

And it was a terribly serious sickness, because Lazarus not only got sick: he also died. The story is in John's Gospel, chapter 11. Martha and Mary sent a message: "Lord, the man you love is ill." And Jesus stayed where he was for two days, enough time for Lazarus to die!

It is a very beautiful story: Jesus always knows

what he is doing. Martha and Mary were shocked because although Jesus knew his friend was sick he didn't do anything about it. Jesus didn't prevent his death, yet Jesus would give him back his life.

What is the greater miracle: preventing death, or giving back life to someone who is dead? Jesus always knows what he is doing.

The only problem is that Jesus doesn't tell us what he's doing... and that gives us cold shivers! We perspire, we feel a rush of adrenaline, and we pass through a tremendous trial, "spiritual stress" and great anxiety! Even though we know he always knows what he's doing, and that he doesn't need to tell us first what he is going to do.

We need to trust, trust, and trust, certain that his love is faithful and that he is always attentive to us, even down to the smallest detail. If we were able to see into the future, we would marvel at the way things are unfolding in our lives. We would say: "What a marvellous thing the Lord is doing! How perfect are his ways! Everything is working out for the best" (see Romans 8:28).

Crooked lines

We know the saying: "God writes straight with crooked lines", but it is not true. It is wrong because God writes straight with straight lines! What is crooked is our eye; it is our faith that is crooked. What is crooked is the way we look at God's ways. God is love, and he always writes straight with lines that are straight: always, always, always! It is not God's lines that have to be changed, nor his way of writing, but our way of looking at how he writes. God is full of wisdom; God is holy. How marvellous God is!

Losing in order to win

I always like to tell the story of the Chinese farmer who had a very good horse on his farm. It was a marvellous horse. His friends came, and said: "Wow, what good luck you have, to have a horse like this on your farm!" And he said: "Good luck? Bad luck? No, nothing like that, God's providence! God knows what he is doing." And the next day the horse ran away. He ran away from the farm, into the forest. The friends came: "What bad luck that your horse ran away…" And he said: "Bad luck? Good luck? No. That doesn't exist – just God's providence. God knows what he is doing." After three months, the horse came back from the forest, bringing wild horses to the farm with him. The farmer had originally lost one, but now he gained a hundred. The friends came: "Wow. You are very lucky, you are a very lucky man!" He said: "Good luck? Bad luck? No, nothing like that. God's providence, yes. God knows what he is doing."

The next day one of the farmer's children went to tame a horse and fell and broke a leg. The friends came: "What bad luck. Your son broke a leg…" And the farmer: "Bad luck? Good luck? God always knows what he is doing! Divine providence." The son was in bed with his leg in plaster. Three days later, the recruiting officers of the Chinese army arrived, conscripting young men for war. They found the farmer's son in bed and so could not force him into the army, and so he did not die in the war. And so the story continues...

Even if you have lost your best horse, even if you have your leg in plaster, don't let yourself say, oh, what bad luck. Say instead, "Blessed be God for my suffering. Blessed be God because my best horse ran away from the farm. Blessed be God that my son broke his leg. Blessed be God that my legs are broken." God always knows what he is doing.

The tears we shed are not something to throw away! They are too precious to be discarded. Let's not forget that the greatest victories are hidden in things that seem to be failures. The cross of Good Friday hid the victory of Easter Sunday and the tears shed at the Lord's Passion made way for the joy of Resurrection. Our sufferings are keys that open the door to a marvellous treasure!

Looking for answers

When they asked Fr Tardif: "Padre, how come when you pray for some they are healed, and when you pray for others they are not?" And he said: "It is true some are, some aren't. That is the first question I am going to ask the Lord Jesus when I get to heaven." And he has already asked that question, because he is already there.

All the servants of God puzzle over the reason for pain and suffering, and all of them look for

answers. No answer is complete, but all help us…
We will see now three reasons for suffering,
suggested by one of these servants of God.

Three reasons

I have a little book that I like to read: *Stories of
Mary, Mother of God.* One of the stories tells of an
experience of Jerome Emilian. He was born in the
region of Venice in Italy in 1486, and became a
soldier, a man of great courage. In the war against
the French during the reign of Louis XII, Jerome
fought valiantly, but the enemy won. Jerome was
taken prisoner and thrown into a cell at the bottom
of a tower. In that dark prison, he saw no chance
of escape, and it seemed he would die there. Feeling
desperate, he thought: "I'll get out from here only
when I'm dead, and after that I'll go to hell," and
he felt terrified. When a person faces up to reality
and has to say, "The next step is death, and after
that, hell", it must truly be terrifying. Jerome
Emilian fortunately remembered his mother, and
the prayers that she had taught him. He prayed to
Mary, trusting in her; he made a vow, promising if
she got him out of there he would go on pilgrimage
to a sanctuary in Treviso. He had not yet finished
his prayer when Our Lady appeared to him saying,
"Don't be afraid, Jerome. Keep your promises and
start a new life!" Our Lady gave him the keys to
the chains that bound him and to the jail. He let
himself out of the prison, hastened to Treviso as a
pilgrim, and left the keys of the jail and the

handcuffs as a testimony on the altar of Our Lady. What an answer Jerome had to his prayer! In the midst of his troubles, a person can come to his senses and see what his situation really means. That can move him to pray with sincerity as never before: "Mother, help me!" "Here are the keys, and change your life!" – because if a sinner is given only the keys to let him out of his prison, that is not an answer, not a solution from God. To take a person out of the jail of sin to continue doing wrong doesn't solve anything. "Here are the keys, and change your life!" And this man changed his life so radically that he became an outstanding example of charity and mercy. He dedicated his life totally to the poor and to the outcast, he founded the Order of Somascha, and today he is St Jerome Emilian.

He has also made a precious contribution to help us understand the mystery of suffering. In his writings, full of wise reflections, he suggests three reasons why God permits suffering: to make us one with him; to make us grow in trust and dependence on him; and to purify us.

First reason:
God wants to make us one with himself

In suffering we are united with God: we become Christ-like in our suffering; suffering brings us closer to God. Jesus invites us, his more intimate friends, to go with him to the cross. Suffering therefore is an effective means of uniting us to

God. How many of us have come to know how much God loves us only after we have been through suffering?

In my Bible I carry a picture of St Francis of Assisi. God has very often spoken to me through that picture. I was going through a time of great suffering: lies were being spread about me and there were many attacks against me. I went to my Bible and it opened where I had put the picture of St Francis. In my heart I heard a voice coming from the picture: "Padre Jorge, welcome to the number of the friends of Jesus." It was a glorious moment for me. All the pain has been worthwhile, because of this one sentence, "Welcome to the number of the friends of Jesus". At that moment I was given a completely new sense of being one with Jesus, and it has remained with me ever since.

Second reason:
God permits suffering to make us grow in trust and dependence on him

Through suffering, we become more sensitive, humble, and dependent. Through the experience of pain we come to see that we have a choice. There are two ways open to us: we can believe, or we can refuse to believe. If we believe, we will live; if we don't believe, we will die.

Isn't that what happens? When we are struggling with a problem, there is a way out that leads to life: faith; and another way out, leading to death: despair. You either believe and live or you don't believe, and die. Either believe and live, or rebel and become depressed, going down into a depression so deep that nobody can take you out of it.

God uses suffering to help us learn to trust more completely and know our dependence on him. Proud, aggressive, inflexible and brusque as we are, we will become dependent, meek, and able to be helped, only when we take the medicine of suffering.

Suffering softens the hard front we put up; the wild horse needs the bridle in his mouth if he is to be tamed. But before he becomes obedient, he needs a few hard smacks on his neck.

Suffering tames us and makes us sensitive, dependent on God, trustful of God, and that is something wonderful.

Cockroaches

Have you seen anyone try to kill a cockroach? It is an insect that is very hard to kill. You hit it away with the broom; it smacks against the wall and falls on its back: dead! But in no time at all, it gets up and comes back running, running around the house. Then you take the spray and squirt it: dead again! It remains "dead" the whole night, but the next morning there it is, all dirty and dizzy, but alive again, walking around the room. It may be dizzy and stumbling, but the cockroach is a stubborn thing. Still alive! So you take a shoe and squash it: its fatty yellow insides come out – "dead" again! But after a while there it is, alive again, squirming and

dragging its own insides around your sitting room…
It may take a good long time before it really dies.

We are like the cockroach: God uses suffering to "kill" us. That is it – to kill the old man in us. Suffering comes, a struggle comes, a difficulty, and we say: "Lord, help me, because from today I will change my life!" After the problem has passed, we continue to behave just as we did before! Isn't it true? And then comes a greater suffering – bad enough to make us very dizzy and disorientated. And again we say: "Lord, now it is for real; help me out of this one, and I will not sin again. I will never get myself involved in that kind of thing again. Help me, Lord, please help me!" And God helps! But once the problem has passed, we carry on doing the very same wrong things. Then we get one of those "treatments", a blow so hard that it "squeezes our insides out". A little more humbly, we pray: "this time it is for sure, now I will change my life. My wife, please forgive me; my children, forgive me. I am going to change my life; I will never again do what I have been doing. Help me; this time I will change my life. Give me another chance". We get a chance, and after a while, still with our insides out, we are back at the same old thing! Isn't that the way things really are? Don't we know someone like that?

Then Jesus comes with a heavy cross and puts it on us, and that cross truly kills us! We die to ourselves, we die to our own ideas, we die to our sin, we die to the world, and our life is hidden with Christ in God (see Colossians 3:3).

Suffering serves to "kill" us for sure. We have to die to ourselves, because otherwise, as we so often do, we play games with God, saying: "Now I have learned my lesson!" Only until the next time – like cockroaches, until we are properly killed, we simply get back to doing things the same old way.

Suffering breaks that in us and makes us humble, dependent and trusting in God.

Third reason:
God uses suffering to purify us

St Jerome Emelian uses gold as an example. Only when it is 24-carat gold, the best, will it stand the greatest heat. What is not gold – the sand and the dross – cannot stand the heat.

Our life is like that: we are precious like gold but there is a good deal of gravel mixed into us. We are precious, more so than gold: we are children of God. That is our greatest treasure; but we carry around plenty of sand and stones inside of us and it takes fire to burn all that out of us – our vices, our sin, our stubbornness, lack of faith, pride, hatred, resentment and many other things.

Not everything in our lives can be washed out with water; for some things, we need fire.

Even today, medicine uses fire in surgical processes, to cauterise wounds.

One of my nostrils was blocked. I spoke with a very nasal voice, and I had difficulty breathing. I went to the doctor and he said: "You have to have the septum cauterised." I asked: "Doctor, are you going to put fire in my nose?" And he answered: "Yes, Padre Jorge, I will use fire in your nose." Then he gave me a local anaesthetic, cut the tissue that was blocking my breathing, and used the cautery to finish off the mini-surgery. There was a smell like a barbecue in my nose, but I was healed.

Many times, only the fire of suffering can heal the deepest wounds we carry around within us. Such suffering is the only way to heal all the sufferings of our lives. It is the suffering that heals.

"My child, this will heal you"

I was about ten years old when my father decided to take us in his car to the farm. The car was a Rural, a real gas-guzzler, and green like an avocado pear.

My father, my mother and Sergio, one of my eleven brothers then living, were in the front seat. In the back seat was another brother, I don't remember which one, Claudio, the youngest of the family, and me. My father was a terrible driver: he could not keep to the road and often drove over the verge. On Sundays when we used to go to Mass, he usually broke off and took along pieces of our neighbours' fences, and the work of the Hermes family on Mondays was to fix up the damage my father had caused with his Rural the day before.

So when we were on the way to the farm, as the poem (I think it was one by Drumond de Andrade) goes: "There was a big stone in the middle of the way, in the middle of the way there was a big stone"... for a change the car was on the road, but my father didn't see the stone, and crashed squarely into it, putting the poor Rural right on top of it! The sudden stop literally threw me out of the car, and on the way I hit my head on the window-handle. It gave me a nasty, long cut, like a line drawn across my head, and it bled copiously. My brother Claudio flew to the front and broke a tooth on Sergio's head.

My mother was worried, because the cut on my head was bleeding without stopping, and she gave me a lot of attention. She took me by the hand and led me to a little crystal-clear stream, and started washing my head, pouring handfuls of water onto my head, saying loving words to me between one handful and the next. I was really enjoying that, because I wouldn't have to go to the farm that afternoon, and besides, all my mother's attention was on me. My head wasn't even sore but I pretended that it was, just to have a little more of her attention for myself alone.

After she had washed my wound, she took me to the house of my brother Rogerio, the eldest of the family, who lived near the farm. She made me sit on a chair and went to the kitchen. In a few minutes she was back, carrying a basin holding a mixture of salt and vinegar, which she poured on my head. How I jumped and screamed! Now it really was sore. I complained and cried a lot, but my mum interrupted: "My child, this is going to heal you for sure!" In fact, very soon a scab formed – a good sign that the cut was in fact healing.

At that early age I understood that not every hurt is healed with water. Some things are healed only with salt and vinegar.

If we sincerely want to be healed by God, we need to allow him to wash us, with water, or when it is necessary, with salt and vinegar.

Chapter 2

Don't waste your tears

The Holy Spirit alone can give us the grace to understand the meaning of suffering in our lives. Let us ask him for light, so that we may not be scandalised by the experience of pain, and able to see the powerful hand of God guiding us through all adversities. It wasn't God who created suffering, although he does use suffering now to serve his own purpose. It's true, you'll agree, that it seems very difficult for God to mould us without pain. Not because God isn't able to do it, but because of the way we are, undisciplined, temperamental, unformed characters, full of bad habits. And because of all that, it is not easy for us to learn what we are taught. Before we take a new direction in our lives, a little pulling of our ears is needed. God lovingly moulds us, using the pain we suffer, like the potter shapes a vase, but only when the clay is well mashed and mixed. Nevertheless God never uses pain unnecessarily. God uses only the pain and suffering needed for our good. God is Love, and he takes no pleasure in sending suffering to his children. It would be a sadistic God who likes to see his children suffer, and not at all like the God revealed by Jesus in the Holy Scriptures – the God who is Love.

The spiritual writer Watchman Nee says that everything that he discovered in God, he discovered only through adversity. And he says, clearly, that we discover nothing new in God unless through the experience of adversity.

Nevertheless, not all suffering makes us grow, and not every adversity brings benefit. What makes us grow is not the suffering in itself, but the way we suffer. An experience of suffering can get us on our feet, or it can cast us down completely – it depends on the way we suffer. There is really great power in suffering, it can either bring us a great blessing or it can take us to utter ruin.

If we pass through suffering in one way, we waste our tears, if we pass through suffering in another way, we benefit greatly.

Let's first see how we can waste our tears and fail to benefit from suffering.

Failing to discover the value of suffering

The Bible speaks about useless, profitless suffering. That kind is horrible. To suffer without profit, without any gain, is pure frustration. It is an absurdity in the full sense of the word. This is what the Book of Wisdom says about those who suffer (3:11): "Their hope is void, their toil unavailing, their achievements unprofitable…" It is an utterly useless kind of suffering. It is a waste of time! To suffer without any gain, suffering that serves no purpose, suffering without profit – how tragic that would be! Suffering itself is already hard enough, but even worse if we gain nothing from it. As a thing without profit, it is disastrous! Who is it that suffers in that kind of way? "But the godless will be duly punished for their reasoning, for neglecting the virtuous man and deserting the Lord. Yes, wretched are they who scorn wisdom and discipline" (Wisdom 3:10).

When is it that suffering is without profit in our life? When is it that we waste our tears? Let us look at a few examples.

Resentment and desire for revenge

We suffer without profit and we shed our tears for no purpose when we suffer with resentment and a blind desire for revenge – when we want to get back at the one we think is making us suffer. If our tears are to be of value, not wasted, we need to get rid of all resentment, all hatred. We need to clear out of our heart all desire to take revenge because if there are such sentiments in us, we will never find freedom, never receive blessing and never be healed.

We may cry a bucketful of tears, but they will be wasted, good only to toss down the drain, if we allow resentment, hatred or desire for revenge to brutalise your heart. Therefore, if that is what is happening, unfortunately we are suffering without profit and wasting a golden opportunity for a real, deep discovery of the love of God in our life.

Being angry and closed up in your own pain

When our suffering makes us become aggressive, scream, lash out, blaspheme against God and offend others, we are "throwing our tears away", and through all the suffering we are nothing but losers. If we do not want this to happen, we simply have to open ourselves more and more to the love of God, and not shut ourselves up in our own pain. Suffering is a tremendous opportunity: it can help us grow and become open to life; it can break cocoons and free us to fly out into wide horizons. If we shut ourselves up in our pain, we will, unfortunately, simply die of suffocation, locked away in ourselves. If we open up to God, we will see "on the far side of the wilderness... the mountain of God" (see Exodus 3:1).

Criticism and pessimism

Many people spill their tears in vain and waste their suffering because they become critical, and keep harping on their own fixed idea that there is something wrong with everything. They become negative and pessimistic; they see only what is wrong, and everything grey. Before they start on any work at all, they are already predicting that it will fail, saying that nothing will come right, that it is no use doing anything because they have tried before and it was all useless... They are constantly finding reasons to grumble, always criticising, and they like to belittle any success anyone else may achieve. They even try everything possible to make sure that things do go wrong, and they enjoy seeing others fail. They are wasting their tears; they are wasting suffering.

Self-pity

There are attitudes that paralyse a person's growth, and one of them is self-pity. Obviously, when we are in pain we cannot deny that the pain is there, but if we make it the most important factor in our life, we ceaselessly whine and fall into an endless spiral of touchiness. And that, of course, leads to feelings of insecurity, fear, misery and inability to trust. If that is the way we are, we will feel bad wherever we may be, distrustful of everything, and thinking that the whole world is talking about us.

Escape mechanisms

We suffer without profit and we throw away our tears when we create escape mechanisms for ourselves and deny reality. People who use escape mechanisms end up creating fantasies and living in an unreal world of pretence, a world of lies. Pay attention here: religion can be simply an escape mechanism for us when we try to use it as a way out of our own troubles, hiding unhealed sufferings under a cloak of hypocritical and corrupt religiosity, trying to cover up conflicts, refusing to face up to our own condition. We run and hide in a world of religious fantasies. When we look for a "hiding-place in religion" without becoming sincerely open to God, our behaviour is immediately marked by symptoms of the vice of religiosity and of abuse of religion. Fanaticism and superstition are two characteristic signs that religion is being used as an escape mechanism. Such spirituality produces a sick mind; it is based on beliefs, not on faith. People in this condition hold on to ready-made formulas and set prayers; they are afraid of speaking freely to Jesus Christ in living faith. Faith is challenging, and those who use escape mechanisms are afraid of looking into their own hearts. If they did, they would have to face up to the reality of their lives. We must be clear about this – it is possible to have plenty of "religion" and very little experience of God, or none at all. People who use escape mechanisms will never be able to overcome their complex, no matter where they hide, unless they take their "reality-therapy" like the prodigal son did, and like alcoholics anonymous do, with humility and in submission to God. Nothing is gained by hiding sufferings and pretending that they are not there. It is necessary to bring them out, expose them to the healing love of God, allowing his light to be poured over the darkness of our soul: "Lord, you yourself are my lamp; my God lights up my darkness" (2 Samuel 22:29; see also Psalm 32:3-7).

Looking for compensation

When suffering comes our way, we often look for something to compensate for it, to relieve the pressure, like an escape valve. Some look for compensation in sin; some turn to vice, hoping to find unbridled pleasure in alcohol, in drugs, in prostitution…

Others look for compensation in the shopping malls: they buy and buy and buy, and not realising that they have become victims of the compulsion to shop.

Others try to find it in food: they eat and eat and eat, and turn into compulsive eaters.

Others turn to gambling: they wager all they have. Spending everything, they lose everything.

Others look for compensation in materialism: they want to own and control more and more and more, and clog up their lives with material things.

Others develop exaggerated attachments, perhaps to another person, perhaps to some thing, and find themselves enslaved by their own affections.

Others try to compensate for suffering by seeking positions of "power". They begin to believe that with a police uniform, or an official appointment in government or in the Church; or a title as leader or coordinator, they will be "immune". They see themselves as above the level of "simple mortals", and believe that they have the right to judge without being judged; to give orders without being accountable to anyone; a law unto themselves. That is how dictators and tyrants are born. Every tyrant is a fragile giant with clay feet (Daniel 2).

Others try to get power for themselves through the occult, through witchcraft, by using magic, or in the esoteric. All that really happens is that they start serving other gods, other lords, and they soon become their slaves (Psalm 16:3-5).

If we try to compensate for suffering in ways like these, we make our suffering simply a way of getting ourselves more and more deeply enslaved. This is very serious. Our suffering turns us into slaves of drugs, of alcohol, of adultery, of prostitution, addicted to violence, to sex, worshippers of idols… Our suffering gives rise to our own enslavement, and that slavery is in turn fed by our suffering: a vicious circle, wasted tears, suffering without profit (Wisdom 3:11).

But let's see how suffering can bring us gain.

Gaining from suffering

Can we gain from suffering? Of course we can! The only reason why God permits suffering is because, through it, we are given an opportunity to grow! We are never tried beyond our strength, and along with the trials that suffering brings we receive the strength necessary to overcome them (see 1 Corinthians 10:13). Often it is possible to get rid of the suffering, and it is in order for us to do that. At other times, we cannot, and what must we do then? It is in that kind of situation that we have an opportunity to gain through suffering!

A sailing boat on the sea is moved by the wind, but the wind doesn't always blow in the right direction. What does the sailor do, then? He has to adjust the sails to be able to move the way he needs to go in spite of the wind against him. If the wind is against him, the sailor needs to tack and tack again, steering a zigzag course first to one side and then to the other, but all the while making headway. We cannot change the wind, but we can adjust the sails! A sail-boat cannot count on always having favourable winds, but it can take advantage of contrary winds and keep on its course!

It is the same with us, we need to adjust the sails of our faith and hope, and the love of God shows us how. We need to surrender ourselves entirely to his holy will and trust that he will never abandon us, and that if he has permitted certain suffering it is only for our good. As we said above, it is not the suffering itself that brings blessing for us, but the way we accept it: that is what makes the difference in any suffering. Accepted, with love, from God, it will be a channel of healing in our lives.

Receiving our tears as a precious gift

"You have noted my agitation, Now collect my tears in your wineskin (see Psalm 56:9). "He… remembers them, he does not ignore the cry of the wretched" (see Psalm 9:12).

Suffering, unfortunately, can be useless. But if in suffering we submit to God and trust him, giving ourselves to him, allowing his powerful hand to mould us, that suffering becomes a source of healing for us and our tears are collected in the wineskin of his merciful heart: "You have noted my agitation, my suffering, and you collect my tears in your wineskin" (older translations say 'your cup').

The suffering that heals is the kind that leads to the tears God collects in the cup of his loving heart. Mary, sister of Lazarus, poured her tears in the cup of God's heart when she came to cry in sadness at Jesus' feet, saying: "Lord, if you had been here, my brother would not have died" (John 11:32,33). Jesus, seeing her tears, wanted to go to the sepulchre where Lazarus was lying in death and the loving presence of God filled that place of desperation and suffering with life, raising Lazarus from the dead. Mary, sister of Lazarus, teaches us to collect our tears in God's cup, crying at the feet of Jesus.

The adulterous woman mentioned in Luke's Gospel (7:36-50), didn't throw away her tears: trustful in the divine mercy, she cried the misery of her sin and of her wretched past at the Lord's feet, and left her tears in God's cup. Her suffering was not useless, her tears were not wasted; on the contrary, through her tears she received the grace to make a new start in her life.

Our sufferings are opportunities: we can cry uselessly and simply try to flush our tears away, or we can cry at the feet of Jesus, and those tears will be saved up in the cup of God's merciful love – the love that always brings incredible graces, blessings and miracles into our lives. And then suffering becomes a powerful channel of healing, freedom and growth for us.

Where do you want your tears to go? Do you want to flush them down the drain? When you suffer with hatred, resentment, desire for revenge, self-pity, desire to kill; when you look for compensation in sin, in vices, in evildoing, and aggressiveness, your tears are, unfortunately, wasted and you are suffering uselessly.

When you turn to God in humble submission and say: "Lord, I didn't choose this suffering but it came! Now I want to gain by it, I want to grow because of it. That is why I come to cry at your feet, renouncing all hatred, all desire for revenge, all bitterness. May my tears and this suffering be a way in my life to discover your love that surpasses all evil and all hatred!" There, your tears begin to be saved, to be collected in the cup of God's merciful heart.

The quarry

I am reminded very much of a verse in the book of Kings: "The building of the Temple was done with quarry-dressed stone; no sound of hammer or pick or any iron tool was to be heard in the Temple while it was being built" (1 Kings 6:7).

Solomon was busy building the Temple in Jerusalem, and for the work he needed a great quantity of stone. The work, and the way it was done, was so perfect that the stones arrived from the quarry ready to be placed in the building. That is why there was no noise of hammering or chiselling or even of smoothing down the stones at the site of the construction.

How wonderful! For the building of the Temple the stones were prepared at the quarry. Our life is the quarry where God is preparing us to take our place in his plan of love for us, and so we can enter into the heavenly kingdom. There will be no need there for hammer, chisel or sanding down to shape and perfect our life.

God has two quarries: one is here on earth, and the other one is purgatory, and I do not want to have to pass through purgatory after this life. That is why I want all the work of polishing done here. All the hammering that I will need I want to be done here; all the chiselling that I need I want God to do here, and all the sanding down necessary to polish and finish this rough stone that I am, I want God to finish that perfect work here, and then, afterwards, he may take me as a living stone and place me in his Temple in heaven.

Our life is the quarry where God is shaping us. Do you know what tools he uses to shape us? He uses suffering as a hammer, as a chisel or as the smoothing tool to break away and get rid of all that is wrong in us, because no rough stones can enter heaven: none at all. No stone in need of polishing can enter heaven.

An author, a contemporary of St Hedwiga wrote about her: "Did you know that living stones used in building the heavenly Jerusalem have to be polished in this world by the wounds we receive, the afflictions we endure, and that many tribulations are needed to pass to the supreme glory of the splendid homeland" (from the Life of St Hedwiga).

God makes use of suffering as an instrument to

purify us. It was not God who created suffering (see Wisdom 1:14), but he uses it to purify us, to cleanse us, to mould us. Our life is the quarry where we are being cut and shaped.

St Paul understood this when he said: "Yes, the troubles which are soon over, though they weigh little, train us for the carrying of the weight of eternal glory which is out of all proportion to them" (2 Corinthians 4:17).

For the person of faith, tribulation becomes the key that opens the treasure of divine glory! Blessed Angela of Foligno used to say, "If we knew the value of suffering, we would be willing to steal it: one would steal the sufferings of another, to benefit from their graces!" St Rose of Lima considered suffering as a weight that we place in the scale to weigh the treasure of grace: she used to say, "Nobody would complain of the cross nor the suffering that come if they only knew in what scale they are weighed out to be distributed to us" (from the writings of St Rose of Lima).

Next, we will look at some of the precious healing that the medicine of suffering brings about.

Healed by the medicine of suffering

When we accept to be healed through suffering, we will at once see a great deal of healing taking place in our life. By the medicine of suffering, God brings forth marvellous fruits in us.

The first fruit:
Suffering breaks down the idol of self

The first fruit of the suffering that heals is the process by which we are taken out of the centre of our own lives. Suffering takes our attention away from self and takes us out of our comfort zone. It destroys the inward idol that we make of ourselves and it breaks all the presumption that leads us to think we have power of our own. Suffering exposes the tremendous irrelevance of self.

Self-centredness is a sign of immaturity. Self-centred people want the whole world to work for them, as though they were the centre of the universe. They are egocentric and closed within themselves. Suffering starts breaking their heart, their attention is taken away from themselves, and they are opened up to receive new life.

The suffering that heals is suffering that takes us out of our egoism, of our self-centredness, of being closed up within ourselves, and it opens our heart to God and to our brothers and sisters.

It is like the butterfly that breaks open its cocoon to come out flying. It struggles inside to be able to use its wings, but that effort is necessary or it will not find the strength to fly. Suffering has this power to take our attention away from ourselves in order to take the "self" from the centre and to allow Jesus to take the place that belongs to him in our heart.

How many people, before the experience of suffering, were closed in within themselves, possessive, egotistic and presumptuous. They thought they were free of problems: "Ha! Not with me. Nothing like that will happen to me, none of the things that happen to others. My family is the best that there is, I feel sorry for the families of other people." Until, that is, something trips them up, and they find out that things can happen to them and their family too. Then they will say: "Hey. Nobody is free of trouble! I'm not going to condemn or judge others."

Suffering takes us out of our comfort zone, takes our attention away from self, and heals us of egoism, attachment to self, and from presumption.

For the life of grace to grow in us, it is necessary for us to surrender the centre of our heart to God. St John the Baptist understood that when he said: "It is important that he should increase and that I should decrease" (John 3:30).

The second fruit:
Suffering makes us contrite and humble, enabling us to serve God

Another thing that suffering brings about in our lives, a marvellous work that it does, is to give us tender hearts. It turns us into people of compunction, contrite, humble, and it gives us docility of heart. "People who are healthy, who have never been hurt, never weak, have little use for God" (J.R. Miller).

Healthy people, not broken, not hurt, have little use for God. They block the way to God's service for themselves and for others. They find themselves so perfect and so much better than the rest of the world … they think they are above average, and they feel they have the right to judge others.

The servants that God loves to use are the ones who have been more broken, more hurt, more wounded. I'm not saying the ones who become resentful, the ones that throw away their tears, but the ones who, accepting their brokenness, enable him to bring about more healing through them: the ones who have been wounded and scourged by suffering.

The great saints are invariably great sufferers. St Teresa of Avila used to say: "If you, Lord God, want to send me suffering, give me strength to suffer and let it come. Here I am." I thought she was exaggerating. But now I understand that she was stronger than suffering, because she was pouring her tears into God's cup; each suffering was an occasion to fill it a little more with her tears, and more blessings flowed out in her life. The great saints were, all of them, great sufferers. They suffered persecutions: from the world, from the devil, from the political powers, from members of their own family, from their brothers in faith, those that should have defended them, from the clergy, from people who were holy and from the impious. They were counted as mad, stupid, brainless, day-dreamers, aliens, insane. They suffered horrors, they suffered prison, exile, defamation, calumny and death. But every suffering would push them nearer to Jesus. And the more they were pressed by suffering, the more the oil of healing would flow from their lives.

Suffering is the oil-press in which the servants of God are pressed in order to allow the oil that heals to be released. The more you press the bunch of grapes, the more the wine flows. The more you press a servant of God, the more the oil of healing is released in his life. This is not simply a poetic image, not just a beautiful thought, it is pure truth. The sufferings that break down our pride leave us contrite, humble, able to be open to others and docile. And the more pressed we are, the better is the wine and oil that flows from us. To draw oil from soybeans, from olives, from corn, from sunflower seed, from peanuts, it is necessary to press them until they are crushed and then press harder. To bring out the "oil of compassion" from a servant of God, it is necessary to press him well.

How many women, housewives, and how many men, heads of families, are there who are pressed every day. How many tears in their eyes: "My son is still avoiding conversion; the more I pray, the further he drifts away!" And they weep, weep, and weep. Don't throw away those tears. Don't waste them. God is collecting them in his cup. You are being pressed. The grace that you are not getting now you will find in the future. You are in the quarry, being cut, shaped, and smoothed, and you are bringing your family to God. Believe this. It is the truth! Don't waste your tears – not ever!

Pray with me: "Lord my God, give me the grace to benefit from my tears, and to grow by my sufferings. May suffering never overwhelm me – not ever. I refuse, Lord, to waste my tears and to waste my suffering: Teach me to weep as a disciple of yours should weep. I want every tear to be blessed by you and collected in the cup of your merciful heart. I want to be more and more like you. Thank you, my God."

The third fruit:
We are emptied of self in order to receive a greater outpouring of the Holy Spirit

Another work that God does in us through suffering is the work of emptying us of self. We need to be emptied more and more of self so that we may receive the Holy Spirit in greater fullness.

See in Romans 5:3-5 what St Paul recommends for you if you are to be a more Spirit-filled person: "These sufferings bring patience as we know, and patience brings perseverance, and perseverance brings hope, and this hope is not deceptive, because the love of God has been poured into our hearts by the Holy Spirit which has been given us."

What a marvellous thing! God has a beautiful recipe for you to receive an outpouring of the Holy Spirit such as you have never experienced before. What is his recipe? Tribulation!

Paul says that tribulation brings patience; that patience takes us to faithfulness; that faithfulness produces hope. Can this hope be deceptive? No! It does not waste our tears. Hope does not deceive because the love of God has been poured into our hearts by the Holy Spirit who has been given us.

If we are to be more filled by the Holy Spirit, the inward spaces of our heart need to be made larger.

Now, listen carefully to what I will tell you: suffering, sadness and pain enlarge the spaces in our heart, and this in turn allows the Holy Spirit more room there. Suffering brings down the walls, breaks the barriers, and destroys the defences we build around ourselves: our human self-assuredness, our reputation, our good name, our impressive image, our successful past, the "references" we are proud of, our religious and our material "pedigree".

Suffering shows that all those things have no value in the life of a servant of God. When you have destroyed all those things that are the source of so much strife in you, you are free to follow God, to receive from God an outpouring of the Holy Spirit such as you have never experienced before.

I can testify to an outpouring of the Holy Spirit coming from the cross (John 19:30) that is simply indescribable. How one's spiritual authority grows! The gospel that we preach is totally different when it flows from that outpouring. The difference is not in the Gospel in itself, obviously, but in the way that it is preached: without beating about the bush, without flowery images, without "lacy edges" (to use an expression of my friend Maria Francisca Longhi of the Oasis Community), nothing spectacular, but alive because you have been living it! It is no use preaching the gospel in any language at all, even the most beautiful, if you don't live it in your own language.

The more Peter was persecuted, the more he was filled with the Holy Spirit. The more he was forbidden to preach the Gospel, the more the Holy Spirit came to him in double doses. The more Paul was scourged, the more the Holy Spirit flowed in his heart.

Suffering empties us of self to prepare us for a greater infilling by God. Many times suffering takes the ground from under our feet: our human self-assuredness and our material wellbeing, the support of others, of our friends, and even the support of the church. Suffering takes away everything.

When that happens to you, you know you don't have any other support but the powerful hand of the Father: "Hold my hand, Lord, hold me, because everything is gone. I am falling into the void!" There is only the hand of my Father and my own conscience. All the things that once gave me comfort are taken away and I begin to depend only on what is essential.

When you have arrived at this point you have nothing else to lose, because you have lost everything. You are never better off than when you have no reputation to defend, for then you can only gain. A servant of God loses nothing because he has already given everything to God; he has surrendered everything to the Lord.

Is it good to suffer? I surely don't like it, because I'm not a masochist. I don't like it and I weep, sometimes I even scream!

But does suffering help? Yes, it does. Many times I go to the cross and I scream: "I want to get away from here", because I don't like to suffer. Suffering is not nice in itself. But though I may scream and cry, I accept the work of God. I come before the Lord Jesus and I say: "Jesus, this really hurts, but cut deeper if you need to. Take the chance while you have it to do all you need to do, for otherwise I may need this kind of surgery again. Your scalpel of suffering has opened me up. Fix everything in me, so that I will not need to go through all the preparation for this operation again. Take the chance; I am open. Do all you need to do, Lord."

Have you ever really been opened up? Did you not feel as though your "insides" were out? When God opens you up, ask Jesus to do all that has to be done: "Do everything, Lord. Change all that has to be changed, Jesus."

Suffering is a channel of healing because it is one of the ways we can experience God. It cuts to the heart, opening it up for a great infusion of the Holy Spirit.

Does it seem that I am trying to convince you not to ask for healing any longer? "Fr Jorge is talking so beautifully about suffering that I don't want to be healed any more. I just want to suffer." Obviously that is not what I am trying do.

I am saying that suffering has no meaning in itself, but for what it can bring us yes, there it has meaning. And maybe Jesus is trying to heal you in a new way, as never before, through the very suffering that up to now you have been rejecting.

Do you understand? Until today you have rejected suffering in your life, and you wonder why Jesus has not taken it away. He has not taken away your suffering, because it is the very thing that will link you to the infinite power of the Holy Spirit of God.

With humble submission, say: "Jesus, I want your hand to mould me. Jesus, I want you to shape me. Blessed be my tears, blessed be my afflictions, blessed be my sufferings, because in the scales of your mercy they are weighing out for me such a great anointing of your Holy Spirit!"

The fourth fruit:
Our hardness is broken and we are made meek

Another marvellous thing that suffering does is that it breaks our hardness and makes us meek.

When you go fishing in the river, you throw in a baited hook. A fish swallows it. As soon as the fish has swallowed the hook, a tremendous battle starts in the water. The fish becomes aggressive and you need a lot of patience to bring it out. Your work will be simply to manage the fishing line, until the fish is tired out. When the fish is exhausted, it comes out meekly. It comes out very meekly.

Many of us are exactly like that: we fight, we are aggressive, we scream at others, until a small hook and line of suffering has been fastened in our chin. Then we become subdued and tamed. Does suffering tame us? Does it? How many people are there who are full of fight, arguing with those around them all the time, until an experience of suffering comes upon them? And the lion that we used to be is transformed into a lamb, that barrel of vinegar is transformed into a pool of sweet serenity: the fighter is tamed! Everyone seeks him out because they feel welcome, loved, they feel at home!

Even as we battle against suffering it tames us. When we set out to tame a horse, it kicks and bucks and neighs a good deal, it fights, but the trainer holds the reins with patience and persistence, and finally the horse allows itself to be mastered! In the same way, suffering tames us.

How many times have we prayed: "Jesus, meek and humble of heart, make my heart like yours!" Jesus hears our prayer – and puts a bridle on us, a bit in our mouth to tame us, to bend our stiff neck. That is what heals! Suffering bends our stubborn will, our hard-hearted desire to remain in control.

The fifth fruit:
We become more human

This is another fantastic work that suffering does: it makes us more human. We get into touch with our own humanness in a profound way. It seems that it is the only way for us to become conscious that we are men and women and not angels! God made us human, not angelic. Suffering lays bare our fragility and shows us our human condition, exposed, and just as it is. That is how the gospel can take flesh in a very deep way in our own life – because we get rid of our spiritual fantasies. We stop living in the clouds, we see ourselves just as we are, bare-footed and profoundly earthly.

Then we discover two great truths: the first is the great misery of the human condition. We are dust and ashes. All presumption of personal omnipotence is destroyed. The idol of self crumbles away to dust and ashes.

The second truth: we discover the infinite mercy of God, who loved this dust, who took it, moistened it with his own breath and used it, moulded us in his own image (Genesis 1:26).

My misery makes me discover the infinite mercy of God. I live with my feet on the ground, conscious of my own humanity, and I discover that God loves me, profoundly, just as I am. And the result of this is that I become able to love and profoundly respect others just as they are. I cannot wish any evil upon them. It is as though they were extensions of my own life. Everything that I want that is good for me, I want for them too. I cannot look at others in anger any more. I cannot do it. I can't look at another as competing with me, but rather as a loved brother or sister with whom I share the grace of God. Suffering makes me more human and makes me look at others with love, respect, mercy and compassion. I can no longr condemn, reject, criticise, or, screaming drive them away.

The sixth fruit:
We gain the inner freedom to let things go

Suffering makes me poor and free in such a way that I am ready to let go of whatever it is that I used to cling to, whether material or spiritual. I am not the owner of truth, of faith, of the church, or of the Bible. We are all heirs of these blessings, heirs of these graces. I don't have to make war and fight tooth and nail to defend my ministry, my position, my honour, because nothing is mine. I am not the owner of anything at all: the Bible is not mine, faith is not mine, the ministry is not mine, life is not mine, the church is not mine, the past is not mine, the present is not mine, the future is not mine. "Naked I came into this world, and naked I will leave it" (Job 1:21). I live naked, with nothing to hide, with nothing to show, to defend, to keep – apart from a good conscience before God. I was born naked and I will leave naked. Everything is a gift of God! Titles, name, fame, reputation, position, repute – they are all worth less than nothing, because those who are baptised are already the greatest thing they could ever be: they are children of God!

The seventh fruit:
We become truly welcoming

Suffering will transform us, making us truly hospitable, ready really to welcome others. I don't have all the answers for your life, but listening to others, my solidarity will make them feel at home in my presence; they will feel loved and welcomed.

The work of suffering makes us human and, humanising us, transforms us and makes us profound and merciful people, understanding, compassionate, good, welcoming, ardently desiring the freedom and good of others.

With Christ we become partakers in his redeeming work, in his cross, and we desire nothing else but the salvation of souls, the good of all people and their immersion in the infinite mercy of God.

The eighth fruit:
Interior freedom

If I suffer, I will be free and I will belong to Jesus Christ and in him, free, I will rise.
St Ignatius of Antioch

Through suffering we become free from every attachment, whether to material things, or to our likes and dislikes, or to things of the spirit, and free too from the dark places within ourselves. We have no need to go any place or to hide anywhere, because wherever we go we are free. Every place becomes our home and yet in every home we feel we are strangers. As we read in a text from the second century that speaks of the way of life of a Christian in the world: "They live in their own country but as passers by; outwardly their life is like that of every other citizen, yet they put up with it all knowing that in this world they do not belong. Every strange country is their own, yet wherever they are they are foreigners" (from the Letter to Diognetus).

The ninth fruit:
Suffering teaches us the meaning of eternity

When we undergo the "treatment" of suffering, we experience more and more the meaning of eternity. We are citizens of heaven (Philippians 3:20; Hebrews 13:14), and we see everything in this world as passing, all is vanishing like smoke (James 4:14; Psalm 39:6-7, 12; Psalm 102:3, 4; Wisdom 2:4-5), only God is absolute, only God is eternal.

Suffering simplifies and unifies. It reduces our lives to the essentials in such a way that we are able to get rid of everything superfluous, everything that is passing, everything that is only apparent and superficial. Our eyes are opened to lasting values, eternal values: love, truth and justice...

As St Paul says, "And so we have no eyes for things that are visible, but only for things that are invisible; for visible things last only for a time, and the invisible things are eternal" (2 Corinthians 4:18).

We become centred on love, and this makes it possible for us to experience more fully God who is Love (1 John 4:8-16). Without a doubt this is the greatest fruit of suffering: that it helps us to be centred in love! When love is central, we let go of vain moralising, vain discussions, disputes, contentions, mediocrities. We discover our "place" in history: alive in love! Wherever we go, the only trace we want to leave of our passing is love. Forgetting about ourselves, we remember love! We pass by; love remains (1 Corinthians 13:8). St Thérèse has a little saying that shows up clearly the true colour of our life: "In the heart of the Church my mother, I will be love".

The tenth fruit:
Suffering makes us courageous

It may seem strange to say it, but it is true: suffering makes us courageous people; it heals us of fear. It is a paradox, for many people become fearful precisely because they have a great deal of suffering in their life. But remember, we are not speaking here of the sufferings and tears that are wasted, but of those that are collected in the wineskin of the merciful heart of God (Psalm 56:9). This kind of suffering takes away our fear. Once we no longer look to our own reputation or claim any credit for our name, when life has quite whittled away the personal image we used to think so important, only then will we be free to accept the way that others see us. We will no longer feel any need to satisfy the world, for we will have no image to preserve, and we will no longer be afraid of being exposed – whether to criticism or to applause – for our life will have been reduced to the essential: centred in the love of God. Our desire will be only to be what God wants us to be: the child he dreamed of when he created us.

The eleventh fruit:
Suffering teaches us to obey

Obedience is one of the most exquisite fruits we can pluck from the tree of suffering. In truth, our salvation and eternal life depend, directly, on obedience to God and to his commandments.

Hebrews 5:8 tells us of the obedience of Jesus to his Father: "Although he was Son, he learned to obey through suffering."

This doesn't mean that Jesus was a rebel, or disobedient, but that his submission to the Father was at the very heart of his approach to the cross and shown forth most clearly in the challenge of the cross. On the tree of the cross Jesus restored the obedience that we had rejected at the tree in paradise. "And in obedience unto death he restored what we had lost by our disobedience" (Common Preface for Sundays). One of the final tests to which a servant of God must submit is the test of obedience. If we obey, we show that we are in the truth; if we rebel, we show that we are not yet prepared or ready.

Obedience to God and to the church is the ultimate weapon against the enemy and his followers, for they refuse to obey God. In this sense, our prayer for freedom is powerful when we are in submission and obedient to God and to the Church.

Without obedience, our worship or our ministry are not acceptable to God. "Is the pleasure of Yahweh in holocausts and sacrifices or in obedience to the voice of Yahweh? Yes, obedience is better

69

than sacrifice, Submissiveness better than the fat of rams. Rebellion is a sin of sorcery, presumption a crime of seraphim (household idols)" 1 Samuel 15:22-23.

The Collegeville commentary on this text explains that the Israelite practice, emphasising ritual rather than obedience to God, was in fact a form of idolatry (p. 275). There are two kinds of idolatry: the first is to adore false gods; the second is falsely to adore the true God. In this sense, if we are not first of all obedient, our worship and ministry are idolatrous practices.

The twelfth fruit:
Suffering confers spiritual authority

One of the most significant aspects of suffering is that it confers a true spiritual authority.

What is the secret of spiritual authority? To allow oneself to be wounded by Christ, for Christ. Satan has a terrible fear of those who are wounded for Christ. When one who is wounded for Christ stands to speak, Satan trembles, for such a one doesn't preach from his mouth only: from every wound the infinite power of God shines forth.

One who knows he is wounded by Christ, or for Christ by something else, for instance sickness or injustice, lives reverently aware of Christ, because every wound is a constant reminder of the healing love of God.

It is worth repeating: the secret of spiritual authority consists in allowing oneself to be wounded for Christ! All the Saints had great spiritual authority, and the saints of today still have great spiritual authority, because they all are wounded for Christ.

Peter and John had tremendous spiritual authority because they bore the wounds of Christ in their bodies (Acts 5:40-42).

Paul had great spiritual authority, because he bore in his own body the marks of Jesus (Galatians 6:17; 2 Corinthians 11:23-33).

In the same way, all the other apostles bore the wounds of Jesus in their lives, and that is why the power of God shines out so effectively in their lives.

The Blessed Virgin also bears the wounds of Christ impressed in her heart (Luke 2:34-35).

The spiritual authority of the Old and the New Testament prophets cannot be doubted, and when we read their lives we can see how much they suffered for the faith (Hebrews 11).

Pope John-Paul II always had great spiritual authority, not just because he was the pope, but because he himself had been wounded for Christ: the seal of his papal authority was bestowed on him on 13 May 1981. We are the disciples of a Wounded One! And "every perfect disciple will be like his master" (Luke 6:40).

When one of Christ's Wounded Ones passes by, everything will be blessed: "When they go through the valley of the Weeper, they make it a place of springs" (Psalm 84:7).

In our day, if we look for spiritual authority to enable us to do the work of our ministries effectively, it is vitally necessary to allow ourselves to be wounded for Christ. We cannot assume authority and act superior to others or as their judges; it is vital for us to welcome our sister humility. Satan greatly fears the humble, but fears not at all those who are bossy, arrogant, or proud, or those that think themselves holy. He doesn't fear such people, because they are already his!

The thirteenth fruit:
Suffering transforms us into a living ministry of healing

Suffering embraced in union with God heals us and transforms us little by little into channels of healing for others. No, it is not only a prayer that heals; it is the life of the person who prays, living all the while caught up in the love of God and so becoming a living ministry of healing. A simple glance from such a person is healing; a word from such a one brings healing; the very way such a one moves among others brings healing; simply by listening, such a person is a healer; a person like that ministers healing by their very way life. A person like that is a living ministry, a ministry made incarnate.

Jesus was the one that healed more than any other because he lived the Passion to the full in his own life. It was not only the prayer Jesus prayed that healed. His hands healed, his glance healed, his word healed; simply by being present, he healed. He did not exercise a ministry, he was a ministry;

healing flowed out from his very presence, from everything he did – because mercy, blessing, forgiveness, grace and peace flowed from his whole being.

The more the body of Jesus was wounded, the more healing love flowed from every wound. The more soil is "wounded", softened to welcome the good seed, the more productive the harvest will be. The more you are wounded, not wasting your tears but drawing closer to the love of God, the more the place where you live, where you are present, will be a place of healing, a place of blessing.

Chapter 3

Wounded and healed by suffering

The life of Job gives us a beautiful testimony, showing how suffering heals and makes Job a living ministry of healing to others. In Job 42:5-6 we read: "I knew you then only by hearsay, but now having seen you with my own eyes, I retract all I have said and in dust and ashes I repent".

This is the way it is with those who are healed through suffering: they are conscious of their human condition; they reject their human myths, their fantasies and all their presumptions. I will try to retell the ongoing story of Job simply, directly, as friends might chat about it.

We know that Job was a God-fearing man, good, just, holy. God himself called him "the just one". The whole world thought he was good, and Job himself believed he was good... Maybe that was his defect.

In those days people believed that God always punished sinners and blessed the just – and there was of course a certain truth in that. But they discovered that it often led to wrong conclusions: it led them to think that if somebody was suffering, he must have sinned, or that at least he could not have been completely honest before God. In the Bible the book of Job is one of the "Wisdom Books". Its subject is about the mystery of the "pains of the innocent": in other words, it speaks of the suffering of the just!

The devil appeared before God (Job 1:6-11) and God asked him: "Where have you been?" And the devil answered, "Roaming about."

God asked him what he had seen on his travels: "Did you see my servant Job? What a good man he is. I am very pleased with that son of mine down there on earth, God-fearing, honest, holy and true." Then the devil asked God an intriguing question: "But Job is not God-fearing for nothing, is he?" Is it for nothing that he loves you? You gave him a beautiful wife, healthy children; he's never sick, he has many friends, a good reputation, money in the bank, large herds on his farms, fantastic harvests. Whatever he does you bless, and everything prospers for him. Treated like that, only a fool would not love you. Take your favours away from him, and see if he keeps on loving you. Do you think that he just simply respects you and expects nothing for it? Of course he expects something in return.

What an embarrassing question that is for us! For the devil does indeed ask us the same question! If God's mercy were withdrawn from us, what would our attitude be! Is there such a thing as disinterested faith? Is there anyone who serves God simply for God's own sake, out of pure love, and seeks no benefit in return, not even heaven?

And God said to the devil, "Very well, do what you like with anything of his, but keep your hands off of his person" (see Job 1:12). That means that the enemy has no permission to tamper with the source of life within us. He has no permission to take our lives. He can tempt us, even to suicide, but he has no divine permission to kill anyone.

God said: "Touch his possessions," and then a real tempest hit Job's life. The word "tempest" appears several times in the book of Job.

And good as Job was, wonderfully God-fearing, correct, prayerful, in one single day he heard that all his sons and daughters had died, his farms had been destroyed, his sheep, his goats, his camels and his cattle all dead, and he himself became covered in sores. The poor man ended up sitting on a dunghill, covering himself in ashes, and there he stayed, depressed, understanding nothing of what was happening to him. Yet he uttered no blasphemy against God.

His wife even suggested a way to put an end to it all, to spite God: "Then his wife said to him, 'Do you mean now to persist in your blamelessness? Curse God and die!'" (Job 2:9).

Three of his friends came to confront him, and to try to explain why he was suffering so. But they really had not a word to say. They stayed for seven days, looking at him without speaking at all. Imagine that scene: those three men, each holding his chin, sitting in that dusty place in the hot sun, quite still and silent, silent…

Many times, in the presence of suffering the

best thing is to keep your mouth shut and say nothing. What is there to say to a mother whose son has been killed today? If you tell her that her pain will pass, it will solve nothing at a moment like that. Certainly she will carry on suffering for a long time, until she is healed of the pain of her son's death.

Job's friends kept quiet for a whole week! Then they started speaking, trying to show Job why it was that he was suffering: "Job, it is like this," one dared to suggest, "You are suffering because you are no good". "What? I'm no good? I'm a good man", insisted Job.

"But Job, only the one who has no sin doesn't suffer, and you are suffering. This proves that you have sinned", the next argued. Job replied. "I agree with you, but still, my case is different. I did not sin."

"Job, there must be an explanation for your suffering", the third said, trying to put another view of the problem.

"But there is none. I'm free of fault, and yet I'm suffering", Job replied.

And the three friends carried on and on making speeches and more speeches, trying to explain suffering according to the theology and doctrine of their time, yet they were unable to convince Job. Ever more convinced that he was innocent and that his suffering was incomprehensible, Job replied: "Everything that you are saying sounds very well from your point of view, but to those who are actually suffering it says nothing. If you were in my place and if I were in yours, I would tell you the same things that you are telling me. I too know by heart all that you are saying, but for one who is actually suffering, like me, it doesn't help at all. Your ideas and the explanations you try to give me are no answer at all to the problem of my suffering" (see Job 16).

It was a long discussion, but the three friends were not able to give any real answer to Job. All their arguments, drawing on the theology, philosophy and moral teaching of the time, could not explain his pain.

Then a young man came along. In those days a young man had no right to speak in the presence of older people, because only the elders were thought to have the wisdom needed for that. But that young man started speaking, and his words touched Job's heart.

That young man presented a new view of what God was like, a new theology, a new vision of the cosmos, a new understanding of the mystery of pain and suffering.

And while the young man was talking, "from the heart of the tempest God gave Job his answer" (38:1; 40:1) revealing to Job how transcendent he is in himself and in his designs, and Job became still. When God spoke to him, he understood everything. And the first thing that showed that he had really discovered the answer, was that Job became humble. He admitted he had been too ready to open his mouth, and he took back all that he had said: he became aware that he was God's creature, utterly dependent, needing to be taught.

I know that you are all-powerful:
What you conceive, you can perform.
I am the man who obscured your designs
with my empty-headed words.
I have been holding forth on matters I cannot
understand,
on marvels beyond me and my knowledge.

(Listen, I have more to say;
now it is my turn to ask questions and yours to
inform me).
I knew you then by hearsay;
but now, having seen you with my own eyes,
I retract all I have said,
and in dust and ashes I repent (Job 42:2-6).

Suffering took Job to a true experience of God: "I knew you then only by hearsay, but now, having seen you with my own eyes…" (vv. 4, 5). Those who have passed through an experience of suffering, not wasting their tears, really do come to a totally new vision of God and of life: the transcendent and the immanent come together.

Once Job had been healed by his suffering, he wa able to become a channel of healing for his friends. God was cross with them, for they had not spoken correctly about Him:

When God had said all this to Job, he turned to Eliphas of Timan: "I burn with anger against you and your two friends… for not speaking truthfully about me as my servant Job has done. So now find seven bullocks and seven rams, and take them back with you to my servant Job, and offer a holocaust for yourselves, while Job my servant offers prayers for you. I will listen to him with favour and excuse you fully for not speaking of me properly as my servant Job has done" (Job 42:7-8).

Job, wounded and healed by suffering, was able to pray for his friends, and through his intercession God blessed them, and did not bring punishment and catastrophe upon them.

Finally, Job got back everything that he had lost in double measure. "The Lord restored Job's fortunes because he had prayed for his friends. More than that, the Lord gave him double what he had before" (Job 42:10).

It is comforting for us to know that on the far side of suffering there is a double measure of blessing waiting for us!

Chapter 4

God's purpose in suffering

This passage from Hebrews, 12:3-13, will help us better to understand the mystery of suffering:

> In the fight against sin, you have not yet had to keep fighting to the point of death.
>
> Have you forgotten that encouraging text in which you are addressed as sons? *My son, when the Lord corrects you, do not treat it lightly; but do not get discouraged when he reprimands you. For the Lord trains the ones that he loves and he punishes all those that he acknowledges as his sons* [Proverbs 3:11]. You are being tried for your correction: it is God that treats you as sons. Suffering is part of your *training*; God is treating you as his *sons*. Has there ever been any *son* whose father did not train *him*? But if you are not getting this training, as all of you are, then you would not be *sons* but bastards. Besides, we have all had our human fathers who punished us, and we respect them for it; we ought to be even more willing to submit ourselves to our

spiritual Father, to be given life. Our human fathers were thinking of this short life when they punished us, and could only do what they thought best; but he does it all for our own good, so that we may share his own holiness. Of course, any punishment is most painful at the time, and far from pleasant; but later, in those on whom it has been used, it bears fruit in peace and goodness. *So hold up your limp arms* and *steady your trembling knees and smooth out the path you tread;* then the injured limb will not be wrenched, it will grow strong again (Isaiah 35:3).

Let's look at verse 11 again: "Of course, any punishment is most painful at the time, and far from pleasant; but later, in those on whom it has been used, it bears fruit in peace and goodness."

The meaning of suffering, according to this passage from the Letter to the Hebrews, is for our correction and discipline, because God loves us and he wants our good. He corrects us because a child without correction is disastrous, a potential delinquent.

Many children have been looked after very well in a material way, but badly educated, because they received no formation for life. And besides education, formation includes the necessary correction. God created us and he gives us the necessary formation and educates us because he treats us as his own children. Quite clearly, you would not want to spend all your time correcting the children of other people when you have your own to bring up. In the same way God, when he corrects us, does it because we are his own children. He does it for our good, to share his life of holiness with us. God didn't create suffering, but he uses the suffering that we all experience to correct us.

Reasons for suffering

Saint Basil the Great (330-379, Bishop of Cesarea in Cappadocia in what is now Turkey), searched deeply into the mystery of suffering, and in his writings leaves us some reasons why God permits sickness and suffering in our lives. He opens up for us several points that I am convinced are very important for us all to know: sickness can serve to discipline and correct us. It may come as punishment for our sins, or as the result of our own negligence, or as sent by Satan. The way we respond to it may serve as an example to those whose faith is weak; its purpose may be to prevent us falling into the sin of pride; and it gives us an opportunity to praise God for the various ways he has provided to help us. We can read of these in *Healing Your Family Tree* by Fr John Hampsch CMF (Queenship Publishing, 1986, pp. 38-39).

One: For correction and discipline

Psalm 119:67: "In earlier days I had to suffer; I used to stray, but now I remember your promise."

Suffering healed the psalmist. "In earlier days I had to suffer; I used to stray, but now I remember your promise". Many times we live a very disorderly life, and as a result we bring all kinds of disgrace upon ourselves. After so much suffering we end up taking a decision to change the way we live and to begin to obey God's commandments. Glory to God!

Psalm 119:71 "It was good for me to have to suffer, the better to learn your statutes."

The psalmist is saying "Thank you Lord for affliction, thank you for pain, thank you Lord for suffering, thank you Lord for tears, thank you Lord for all the difficulties that you use to correct me. Before suffering this affliction, I used to behave sinfully and I was far away from you. But now affliction has corrected me; it healed my heart; suffering healed me. Thank you Lord!"

I like to watch a blacksmith at work. He takes a piece of iron, puts it into the fire to heat it, and then he holds it on the anvil and hammers it until it takes the shape he wants to give it. With fire and with the hammer, he gives the iron the shape he wants for it.

That is our life: first thrown in the fire of suffering and then receiving the "hammer blows", we find our ideas shaken up and we begin to understand. Is it not so? Many times only with affliction and suffering will we be able to learn.

We make many mistakes:
- we live like libertines and contract a disease;
- we make dishonest deals, and people stop trusting us;
- we avoid paying what we owe, and we lose our good name;

- we use our credit card beyond the limit, we buy what we can't afford, spend money we don't have, the bank closes the card account and today we can't get credit anywhere;
- we criticise someone, bear false witness, and remorseful now, our conscience gives us no peace; we have nightmares, and people call us gossips;
- we betray a friend, we are false to him, we break confidence, and we are burdened by the guilt of it...

All of that serves as a lesson to us, not to fall into such mistakes!

Broken so that we can function properly

A famous violinist, very well known for the beauty of his playing, was most demanding when it came to the quality of his instrument. He made an arrangement with the very best of violin-makers to provide him with one. On the agreed day he went to fetch his instrument, and when he started to test it, still in the factory, he touched the strings lightly, frowned, and because he did not like the tone, smashed the violin down on the table, breaking it to bits. He took out his wallet, opened it and put the price of the violin on the table, and went off. Some time later he went back to the violin-maker's workplace and saw a violin on the table. He picked it up to test its quality, touched the strings lightly, and found its tone exquisite. He spoke to the violin-maker: "This one. Yes! This is the one I want. How much?"

"You've paid for it," was the answer. "This is the one that you broke to pieces. I put it together again, and this violin that you now hold is the result. It is yours. You may take it!"

Many times we only function properly after we have been broken, taken apart. While we are still in one piece, body and soul we are subject to sin. Lovingly, God allows the experience of suffering to break us, shattering our life, pieces all over the place! Once broken like that, God puts us together again as a new person!

Two: Punishment

Suffering can also serve God's purpose, St Basil the Great says, as punishment for sin. It is not God who punishes us; it is our own sin that brings punishment on us (see Proverbs 8:36). "For the wage paid by sin is death" (Romans 6:23), that is, if it is in sin that we sow, it will be death that we reap. Basil the Great helps us to be aware that by our own sins we can bring pain and suffering upon ourselves.

It will help us to remember and ponder upon these passages in the Word of God: "I, for my part, say, Yahweh, take pity on me! Cure me, for I have sinned against you" (Psalm 41:5). The Psalmist is saying: "I am sick because of my sin. I need you to heal me because I have sinned against you. My sin is the cause of my sickness, my infirmity, and of many disturbances in my life."

Many things that are not going well in our lives will only change after we deal with sin by repenting, confessing, and amending our ways. "In forgiving all your offences, in curing all your diseases." (Psalm 103:3).

Again we see the connection between forgiveness and healing. God forgives sin and heals the person who is sick.

Psalm 107:17 – "Some driven frantic by their sins, made miserable by their own guilt, and finding all food repugnant, were nearly at death's door."

Many of those who are sick, feeling as though they were at death's door, would find a good confession a great relief, a healing experience.

This obviously doesn't mean that every time you're sick it's a direct result of a sin that you cling to and refuse to give up. Yet it is a fact that many people are sick because of a sin they have not yet dealt with, and they will not be healed unless and until they have a change of heart, repent of the sin and confess it. No medicine, no surgery, cures the problems that stem from our sins except only the remedy of God's forgiveness.

Isaiah 33:24 – "No one living there shall say 'I am sickly'. The people who live there will be forgiven all their faults."

See here, again, the strong link between forgiveness and the healing of a particular suffering? Have you thought what would happen if everybody decided to repent, confess, and change their lives? Have you thought what would happen if an entire city decided to close immediately: if all the places of businesses that trade on sin and at the same time all the people did penance for their sins? If all the erotic shows were cancelled? If all the places where the occult is practised were closed down? If all the bosses paid their employees a just salary? If all the workers worked faithfully, diligently? If all illicit business were banished? If all adultery stopped? If husbands and wives, loving each other, kept away from all infidelity? – how families would be blessed! If all, especially young people, abandoned drugs, promiscuity and violence? If the wicked practice of abortion ceased? If hatred and resentment and desire for revenge were banished from all our hearts? If jealousy and envy and egoism, selfishness, lying, falsehood, hypocrisy, judgmental attitudes, calumny, defamation, oppression and all other sins were eliminated? If power and money were never used corruptly? If all politicians carried out their mandate with honour? Do you think that this is a crazy dream? Jesus had that dream when he died for us on the cross!

The Second Book of Kings tells of a serious sin committed by King Ahaziah. "Ahaziah had fallen from the balcony of his upper room in Samaria, and was lying ill; so he sent messengers, saying to them, 'Go and consult Baalzebub the god of Ekron and ask whether I shall recover from my illness'."

While the messengers were on the way, the prophet Elijah came to meet them, and said, "Is there no God in Israel for you to go and consult Baalzebub the god of Ekron" to ask him whether the king will get well or die?

"Go back to the king who sent you, and tell him this: the bed you have got into, you will not get out of. You are certainly going to die." The messengers went back to the king, who asked them why they had come back so quickly.

They answered him that they had met a man on the way who sent them back with a message that the king will die.

The king asked, "Who is that man?"

"We don't know who he is", they answered, "but he has a very severe face, and is dressed in carnel skin, and there is authority in his voice…"

"It is Elijah! It is Elijah!" the king exclaimed. "Bring him here. I want to show him… I want him to know if this is the way to treat the king."

Elijah was sitting on a rock on the top of the mountain. Ahaziah sent a captain with fifty men, and they said: "Come down, man of God; this is an order from the king!"

"If I am a man of God", said Elijah, "let fire come down from heaven and destroy both you and your fifty men." And fire came down from heaven and destroyed him and his fifty men! That was a fiery prophet!

Ahaziah sent another captain with another fifty men, the very same thing happened to them as to the first lot.

He sent a third captain with another fifty men. This captain pleaded humbly for mercy: "My Lord, let my life and the lives of these fifty servants of yours have some value in your eyes. I am only obeying orders from the king; don't call fire down on me and these men. Please will you be so kind as to come down and speak to the king. 'Very well. Let's go', said Elijah."

When they arrived at Ahaziah's house, Elijah said, "Since you send messengers to consult Baalzebub, the god of Ekron… you are certainly going to die!" (see 2 Kings 1:1-16).

Clearly, this king was a tragic symbol of Israel as a whole. Israel's king died – the nation was doomed – because of idolatry. Without a doubt the sin of idolatry is the cause of a great deal of sickness.

Romans 2:9 – "Pain and suffering will come to every human being who employs himself in evil."

There are many people heavily troubled in conscience because of the evil they have done and because of the sin they keep hidden. Tribulation and suffering come to all those who do what is evil. Such people will not sleep easy however soft and comfortable the pillow, or good the bed, as long as sin is hidden in their heart.

Sin "shortens God's hand" (see Isaiah 50:2, 59:1). How many people there are who plead again and again for healing, but leave an open spout spewing filth and more filth into their heart! If your sink has accidentally run over and you want to mop up the water on the floor, the first thing you do is turn off the tap. If you leave the water running, you'll be working in vain and wasting time trying to dry the floor. Just so, if you want to find freedom and healing, the first thing you have to do is to turn off the tap of sin and let no more filth into your life.

This very same lesson is given us in the book of Ecclesiasticus 38:9-12: "My son, when you are ill… pray to the Lord and he will heal you. Renounce your faults… then let the doctor take over…"

This shows us three things to do when we are sick: pray, ask God to forgive you, and consult the doctor. If we take medicine for a bodily ill without caring for our spiritual health, we will be spending a lot of money but find no improvement in our health. Many sick people experience no change, no recovery, chiefly because they do not deal with their sin. That is why their sickness remains, and they will carry on spending, to the last penny, without finding a solution for their problem.

Three: Our negligence

Basil the Great suggests a third reason why we get sick: we are negligent, we don't take care of ourselves – in other words, the reason is our own human failure. For example, someone starts smoking and develops a serious lung condition, cancer perhaps. Another takes to alcohol and his health is badly affected, cirrhosis of the liver perhaps. He also brings count- less problems on himself, his marriage and his family. Another, follows a dissolute lifestyle and contracts a possibly fatal condition, AIDS perhaps. Is that because God is punishing him? Not at all! He himself triggered all of his trouble by abusing his freedom.

It has often happened that an entire town falls victim to a sickness, simply because those respons- ible for the sanitary facilities don't do a proper job;

they don't keep things clean, they leave sewers wide open… Pain and sickness, misery and suffering, are very often due to nothing more than human negligence.

Hunger is a clear example of this kind of negligence: there are six billion of us living on this earth. Every year we harvest enough food for eleven billion human beings. How is it possible to justify the fact that 800 million people, our brothers and sisters, are dying of hunger in our day?

A great part of the trouble and confusion that plagues our life could have been avoided if we had made the right choices. We know that something is not good for us, but we persist in wanting it, and we end up bringing trouble and confusion on ourselves for the rest of our days.

A young woman knows that this fellow is no good for her, but she goes ahead and marries him anyway! Result: she suffers for the rest of her life.

A young man starts drugging himself. He will reap the consequences of his vice.

God does not bless the wrong things we do. God does not bless sin, for sin "shortens his hand".

Four: Sent by Satan

Basil the Great says that sickness and suffering can be sent by Satan. Many sufferings, many infirmities and other difficulties will be healed through prayer for deliverance or through exorcism. Sometimes prayer for inner healing is needed, asking God to deal with old wounds and traumas that remain in us, that the enemy is using to enslave us.

In a different kind of way, God has sometimes allowed demonic attacks on his servants: like Job, the apostle Paul, Padre Pio of Pietrelcina, Don Bosco, and many others. In that kind of situation, there is no need of prayer for deliverance, and of course exorcism was not called for. They experienced what they did by a very special divine permission, through which they could grow in holiness, and learn to feel in their own life the atrocities the enemy inflicts. The attacks they endured gave them an ability to help others, and helped to cast light on the mystery of evil in the world.

Many sicknesses come upon us, however, because we leave a door open to the enemy. God does not want the enemy to oppress your life or the life of your family. That is why we should turn to the Lord with a humble heart and plead with him to deliver us from the powers of evil and set our life free. Jesus so much wants this, that in the Our Father he teaches us to ask for two things against evil: "forgive us our offences", referring to our own personal sins, and "deliver us from evil", referring to the spiritual vexations that the evil spirits bring upon us. The Eucharist, the Sacrament of Reconciliation, devotion to Our Lady, and striving after holiness of life are wonderful ways to find deliverance from the snares of the enemy.

When we are dealing with the action of the enemy, we must be able to recognise it: is it by special permission of God, as in the case of Job and St Paul and other saints, or is it one of the countless actions of the enemy, simply malicious? We need to be able to tell the difference. If it is something God has permitted, there is no call for a prayer of deliverance or exorcism – that would be wholly inappropriate, and not possible. If it is from the enemy's malice, we need simply to banish it from our lives.

Job, Padre Pio, St Paul and Don Bosco did not live in the world of sin and of darkness: they didn't go in for witchcraft, spiritism, numerology, horoscopes, Tarot, astral mapping, mental telepathy, ouija boards, gnomology, clairvoyance, magic rituals or any of the many other things forbidden by God in the Scriptures (Leviticus 19:31; 20:6,20,27; Deuteronomy 18:9-14, etc).

If on the other hand anybody is practising spiritism, divination, throwing the bones, witchcraft and other esoteric and demoniac practices, then this person keeps a door open all the time to the evil one and will be oppressed by the devil; the devil will enter and take over that person's life. If you want to be free of confusion don't have other gods in your life, for there are many sufferings in store for those who adore them (see Psalm 16:4). If you do not adore the true and only God, but follow the way of darkness and the occult, you are welcoming, encouraging and worshipping the author of disgrace and unhappiness, Satan himself.

I repeat: Padre Pio, Don Bosco, and other saints whom God allowed to be tormented by the devil, were saints who adored the living God, lived a holy life and did not practise any false cults. On the other hand many people are suffering today from the attacks of the devil because they really do give themselves to false cults, and besides, in their hearts they cling to sin, hatred, resentment, their hurts, their desire for revenge, the lies they tell of others, their desire to ruin the good name of others, and because of that sickness comes, and the enemy makes use of those things to make their lives a living hell.

Five: Example to the weak

There is another reason why God permits suffering: it allows one to be an example to those whose faith is weak.

There are many who ask: so-and-so is so good, he serves the community, he is faithful to God, and yet he suffers so much. What kind of God allows that?

He is such a good God that he gives one who is faithful to him an opportunity to help another whose faith is weak. Many holy and devoted people suffer to serve as an example to another who is weak in faith, so that when a trial comes upon the weak one, he should not be scandalised, but see how the faithful one faces pain and difficulty, and draw strength to stand firm himself and be just as faithful to God.

Six: Prevention of pride

Another reason for suffering that Basil the Great points out is: prevention of pride. There is a passage about that in 2 Corinthians 12:7-10 that gives us the picture very clearly and unmistakably.

Saint Paul says,

> In view of the extraordinary nature of these revelations, to stop me from getting too proud I was given a thorn in the flesh, an angel of Satan to beat me and to stop me from getting too proud! About this thing I have pleaded with the Lord three times for it to leave me, but he has said, 'my grace is enough for you: my power is at its best in weakness.' So I shall be very happy to make my weakness my special boast, so that the power of Christ may stay over me...

Saint Paul was a man greatly enlightened by the Holy Spirit, full of gifts and charisms, and endowed with marvellous courage. In spite of it all, he was easily inclined to be proud. That is why God permitted the angel of Satan to beat him, and in that way free him from the danger of vanity.

If all the problems of St Paul's life had been solved, pride and vanity would have become a great problem and a great risk to him. With no problem to solve, he would have run the risk of falling into pride and nobody would have been able to put up with him. In verse 10 he says, "And this is why I am quite content with my weaknesses, and insults, hardships, persecutions, and the agonies I go through for Christ's sake. For it is when I am weak that I am strong." Paul's suffering was the kind of suffering that heals. His suffering was permitted for one purpose only: to free him from the danger of vanity and pride.

I know many servants of God who witness to Jesus with their lips and with their lives, but they still have to go through great problems and difficulties in their families. Children who go astray, children who don't serve God. It seems that this kind of situation arises in order to prevent a person becoming filled with pride, presumption, vanity, and so to fall from grace.

I know people who have a tremendous healing ministry in spite of the fact that they live with sick people for whom they have prayed many, many times and who it seems have never been healed of anything at all! A root of personal vanity would easily begin to grow if every time we pray for someone to be healed that person was healed. To prevent us falling into that kind of vanity, God always leaves us in situations that remain unsolved, so that we don't forget that we are dust and ashes, not almighty wonders able to solve all problems. God knows what he does.

It is patently true: we certainly remain humble when we don't have all our problems solved. That is why I can ask you to pray with me: "Thank you, Lord, for the problems that are not yet solved, because they are helping to solve other problems in my life".

Another reason: to praise God for the resources that he left to heal us, the material ones as well as the spiritual ones.

What a marvellous resource is medicine! Praised be God for the development of medicine! We can say that medicine today works real miracles.

A friend of mine had a serious accident in the south of Brazil and was left with his skull badly broken and his brains out of place. He was taken to a local hospital where they removed a fragment of the skull and put it in the fridge. After that, my friend was moved to the Albert Einstein hospital in Sao Paulo, much better equipped with medical resources. But the piece of his skull was left behind in the south. After a few weeks of treatment, he regained consciousness but, although he was over 20 years old and a university student, he had reverted to the mental age of a three-year-old. He could not remember a thing about his life. At that stage, the missing bit of his head was brought from the south of Brazil and re-implanted. With a little more treatment his adult mind was restored, his memory returned, and in the space of a little more than a year he returned to his studies. A little while later he graduated and today lives a normal life and suffers hardly any consequences of the accident. If that had happened some time ago, medicine would not have had the requisite resources and my friend would probably have died.

Praised be God for medicine, for the discovery of new remedies and vaccines, for the new techniques of surgery. Thank God for all of those things, for they open the way for the children of God to enjoy good health. The book of Ecclesiasticus, chapter 38, gives great honour to the doctor and to medicine when it says that God created herbs with which man may make ointments that are good for our health. It was not man, but God, who created the things we use as remedies. Yet man "invents" remedies, discovering formulas that make it possible to make medicines. God is the creator of the chemical elements indispensable to the making of the medicine.

What are we to say of resources in the field of mental health? Praised be God for the advances in psychology and psychiatry that help to solve so many conflicts in the human mind!

What are we to say of the resources of a sincere and faithful friendship? Praised be God for the friends we discover when we are in the midst of an experience of pain and suffering! What a marvellous gift God gives us through our friends and their sincere and unconditional friendship! We would never have really known what it was to have true friends if it were not for the experience of pain. How welcome is a friend when we are suffering, when we are misunderstood, when we have been hurt by the cruel lies told about us, and the damage done to our good name! How that friend turns out to be Jesus for us! He makes himself present like the good Samaritan: bending over us, tending to our wounds, welcoming us into the inn of his heart; spending the coins of his time, his presence, his intercession; and above all of his unconditional acceptance and understanding that doesn't accuse or reprimand us because he knows that when we experience pain we are more in need of an embrace than of a sermon.

When we discover a friend in the midst of our pain, he comes to us like fresh water to a thirsting heart. Such a friend is the presence of Jesus himself to us. When we can no longer walk, he lends us his legs. When we are weak in faith and trust, he believes and waits in our place. When we cannot speak, he speaks for us. When we are bent by suffering, he holds out his hand to lift us up. When anger stirs strongly in us, he understands. When we are not feeling well, he seems to know, and right away he phones, writes, or comes to visit: "A faithful friend is a sure shelter: whoever finds one has found a great treasure. A faithful friend is something beyond price, there is no measuring his worth". Gold and silver are nothing in comparison with the sincerity of a friend's faith. "A faithful friend is the elixir of life, and those who fear the Lord will find one" (see Ecclesiasticus 6:14-16).

What are we to say about the resources of a Christian community? How many of us, because of pain, discover a prayer group, a Christian fellowship, a group of people who love God passionately and love us sincerely and are interested in us and in our spiritual growth! How many of us, precisely because of pain, became aware of baptism in the Spirit; discover how to praise and adore the living God and find that we can open ourselves to the experience of God's love, coming to know so many charisms of the Holy Spirit, the Sacraments, healing ministries – marvellous resources that God left in his Church to heal us?

Our infirmities were the bait God used to "fish" for us and bring us to live the kind of life we are living today. Our sufferings are what led us to praise God and celebrate his glory.

Chapter 5

How we should suffer

As we have already said, suffering has no meaning
in itself, but as to where it takes us, it certainly
does have meaning. It is the way we suffer that
makes the difference. Suffering is no good, but
what great good it can do!

In the battle with suffering, the game will not
end in a draw: either we win or we lose! I can
testify that the greatest blessings I have received in
my life came to me hidden in the treasure of the
cross, and suffering was the key that opened the
door to the Treasure!

The word of God teaches us the right way to
suffer. Let's see 1 Peter 2:19-24:

> You see, there is some merit in putting up
> with the pains of unearned punishment if it
> is done for the sake of God. But there is
> nothing meritorious in taking a beating
> patiently if you have done something wrong
> to deserve it. The merit in the sight of God,
> is in bearing it patiently when you are
> punished after doing your duty.

This, in fact, is what you were called to do, because Christ suffered for you and left an example for you to follow the way he took. He had not done anything wrong and *there had been no perjury in his mouth.* He was insulted and did not retaliate with insults; when he was tortured he made no threats, but put his trust in the righteous judge. He was *bearing our faults* in his own body on the cross, so that we might die to our faults and live for holiness; *through his wounds we have been healed* [Isaiah 53:5].

Jesus, says St Peter, left us an example that teaches us how to suffer (see 1 Peter 2:21) – the word "example" is a translation of the Greek word *hypogrammon* meaning "according to the letter", which the disciples were to copy: that is, according to the authority of the Master. When I learned to write, the custom was to imitate the examples of the letters all printed in beautiful script in a book. My first teacher, actually my sister, Terezinha, wrote out a word or a phrase using that script and told me to copy it several times until I had learned to make my writing very like her own. Jesus, in the same way, left an example, the model of how we should suffer that we may suffer like him and not throw away our tears. There are three dimensions to the example Jesus left us: how to relate to ourselves, how to relate to others, and how to relate to God.

How to relate to ourselves: innocence

The servant of Yahweh was harshly dealt with, "though he had done no wrong and there had been no perjury in his mouth" (Isaiah 53:9).

The more innocent we are, the more our suffering will be blessed and will serve to bless others. To harvest the precious blessings of suffering, it is necessary not to seek to justify ourselves but to be justified in Christ Jesus, so that we may suffer as innocently as possible. It is clear that strictly speaking only Jesus suffered unjustly because there was no sin in him, whereas none of us can say that our sufferings are entirely unjust and therefore innocent.

The first thing I should do when suffering comes is to do penance and confess, so that I may be cleansed of my sins. My suffering may be deserved or undeserved it doesn't matter. The first step is penance and confession. Always, when someone says something bad about me, persecutes me or calumniates me, the first thing that I should do is to humble myself under the powerful hand of God (see 1 Peter 5:6), recognising that I am a sinner and that I need to ask God's forgiveness.

If you are going through some form of suffering, sickness, trial, be it what it may, look first of all to repenting of your own sins and confess, in order that your suffering may be as innocent as possible. To make suffering a blessing, the first secret to learn is to be contrite of heart.

How to relate to others: blessing

"He was insulted and did not retaliate with insults; when he was tortured he made no threats." (1 Peter 2:23). The second thing that I should do if I want to suffer in holiness is to renounce vengeance. Rather, "Love your enemies, do good to those who hate you, bless those who curse you, pray for those who treat you badly" (see Luke 6:27-28). I must confess that this is not an easy thing to do. When somebody treats us badly, betrays us or defames us, strange feelings rise up within us: confusion, rage, shame, humiliation, fear, insecurity, desire to run away, self-pity. We perspire, we experience cold shivers, we cannot sleep, we lose our appetite, we get an upset stomach, we lose our zest for life – all kinds of bad, very bad feelings indeed! Our blood "boils" and we want to take revenge.

Let me share with you what I do when I begin to feel this desire to take revenge on someone who has made me suffer: I fast and pray for that person until the desire to take revenge is converted into compassion for that person. It is not easy but it works.

Henri Nouwen says that we have in us a "compulsive I" that needs to be changed into a "compassionate I". This process of transformation is slow and painful, but when finally we understand that our compulsions are transformed into compassion, our joy is indescribable! We start living in a place that is beyond suffering.

If we are to be able not to threaten those who treat us badly, the secret is to obey God's word that says: "Never pay back one wrong with another, or an angry word with another one; instead pay back with a blessing. That is what you are called to do so that you inherit a blessing yourselves" (1 Peter 3:9).

Instead of throwing insults at the ones that do wrong to us, we should send a blessing to them, and we will be "heirs" of the blessing. Our heart will not become hardened; on the contrary, it will turn out to be meek and peaceful. We ourselves will be the first to benefit from our own meek and peaceful heart.

How to relate to God: in sacrifice of praise

"He put his trust in the righteous judge" (1 Peter 2:23).

God is our "sure place", our rock of refuge, in the midst of pain and suffering. Everything can be shaken and the floor under our feet may become like shifting sand, but the Father's arms are always strong, tender, welcoming, firm ground, an impregnable fortress, a secure refuge where we will find shelter!

So let us not surrender ourselves to sorrow and pessimism, but rather surrender ourselves into the hands of God. That is the difference between useless suffering and suffering that is blessed. If I surrender myself to hatred or desire for revenge, my suffering is useless, suffering without profit. If I surrender to God, my suffering is blessed, happy suffering! Yes, happy suffering because it is what made me surrender myself into God's loving hands. I say again what I said above: in the battle with suffering the game is never drawn. If I surrender myself to resentment I am the loser; if I surrender myself to God, I am the winner!

Jesus gave us the example. His last words on the cross were, "Father, into your hands I commit my spirit (Luke 23:46)". And the result of that commitment into the Father's hands was that three days later Jesus was alive! The secret of triumph over suffering is to surrender ourselves into the Father's hands. Maybe our suffering is bigger than ourselves, but the Father is bigger than the suffering! Whenever I surrender myself to the Father, suffering is transformed into blessing, the cross is transformed into resurrection, sadness is transformed into joy, fear is transformed into courage, and doubt is transformed into hope, a compulsion is transformed into compassion, and death is transformed into life!

One of the things that gives most glory to the Father is our sacrifice of praise. That means, from the midst of our suffering and pain, we offer ourselves to God in an oblation of love and adoration!

"Now my soul is troubled. What shall I say: Father, save me from this hour? But it was for this very reason that I have come to this hour. Father, glorify your name." Jesus was about to suffer the Passion. He said his soul was troubled and saw that he had two options: one, to ask the Father to save him from it; and the other, to offer himself to the Father so that the Father's name would be glorified. Jesus chose the second, and… "a voice came from heaven, 'I have glorified it, and I will glorify it again'" (see John 12:27-29).

In the experience of pain, we have two possibilities: we may try to escape from it at any cost; moaning and groaning, shouting, full of resentment. Or as a sacrifice of praise we can abandon ourselves into the loving hands of the Father so that he may do what is best and his name be glorified. Jesus gives us the guarantee that we can indeed abandon ourselves into the Father's hands because the Father loves us. He is faithful, he knows what he is doing, he never fails to fulfil his promises and he raises up those who, in the midst of the cross, surrender themselves to him.

Conclusion

Jesus wept, and he invites us to weep too (John 11:35; Luke 23:28).

Twice the Gospels tell us that Jesus cried: at the death of Lazarus (John 11:35), and on the Mount of Olives, when he felt how hard the hearts of the children of Jerusalem were (Luke 19:41-44).

Jesus cried on account of two realities of the human condition: death and sin. In truth one reality only – because sin is the most horrific form of death.

Our God cries for his people. Idols don't cry because they have no feelings, they have no life. An idol has no blood; it needs the blood of its victims. That is why the idols enslaved their devotees. They need their blood.

Jesus cried because he has blood, he became flesh, he lived among us (John 1:14). Jesus has blood, feelings, he is moved by compassion! He cried for us, cried over us, and cries with us. He is Immanuel, God with us, and he came to cry with us. His tears of love fall over us to wash us, to cleanse, to purify, forgive and heal us. He was upset at the tears of the poor widow of Nain (Luke 7:13) and he took the initiative, miraculously raising up the young man although no one had asked it of him: he is the God of Consolation, and his compassion makes him anticipate our call for help. His innocent glance provoked tears in Peter (Luke 22:62); he consoles the tears of the Magdalene (John 20:11-18) and consoles the disciples' weeping as on the day of the Resurrection (Mark 16:10).

As the Incarnate Word (John 1:14), and as the Living One (Revelations 1:18), he continues in our midst. Sometimes he invites us to cry (Luke 23:28), and at other times tells us not to cry (Luke 7:13), asking the reason why we cry (John 20:15). Assuring us that our crying and sadness will be changed into joy (John 16:20), consoling us, blessing our tears (Matthew 5:4), drawing us into his eternal life and promising that

> the One who sits on the throne will spread his tent over them. They will never hunger or thirst again, neither the sun nor scorching wind will ever plague them, because the Lamb who is at the throne will be their shepherd and will lead them to springs of living water; and God will wipe away all tears from their eyes (Revelation 7:15-16).

We are on our way to a new heaven and a new earth, beyond suffering, where God our Host is waiting to welcome us to his tent so that we can live together forever. "He will wipe away all tears from their eyes; there will be no more death and no more mourning or sadness. The world of the past has gone" (Revelation 21:4).

And then our tears will be fulfilling their mission,
and they will be kept eternally
in the cup of God's merciful heart.